Berlitz®

Croatia

D0318508

Front cover: Rovinj old town and
waterfront
Right: Sculpture of Bishop Grgur
of Nin by Ivan Meštrović in Split

Basilica of Euphrasius in Poreč. The mosaics here are superb examples of Byzantine art. See page 47.

Dubrovnik. This stunning city has been dubbed the 'Pearl of the Adriatic'. See page 70.

Rab Town. A quintessential coastal town is found on the island of Rab. See page 57.

Tvrda. The old quarter of Osijek has fine Baroque architecture. See page 40.

Roman Amphitheatre in Pula. Once known as Polensium, the city is home to Croatia's top archaeological site. See page 42.

Diocletian's Palace. A remarkably intact Roman complex in Split. See page 66.

Plitvice Lakes National Park. Comprises a chain of 16 lakes linked by waterfalls. See page 37.

Mljet National Park. With two stunning lakes, Mljet in Southern Dalmatia reflects the beauty of Croatia's coastline. See page 80.

St Donat's. This cylindrical church is one of several fine places of worship in Zadar. See page 61.

Paklenica National Park. Popular for climbing and hiking. See page 56.

A PERFECT TOUR

Day 1 — Pula

Fly into Pula and wander around the magnificent Roman amphitheatre. Treat yourself to some pampering and an overnight stay at the Valsabbion (see page 136), where you can admire the panoramic views from its top floor spa.

Day 4 — Šibenik and Krka Falls

Spend the night in style on one of Croatia's smallest islands, Krapanj. On your way, take lunch in delightful Šibenik and visit the Bunari museum. Then head for the magnificent Krka waterfalls.

Day 3 — Zadar

Stay overnight in Sukošan. Head to Zadar in time to see the sunset and the sound and light show. Enjoy the entertainment at the Garden or Arsenal nearby.

Day 5 — Trogir

Take the coast road to Trogir, stopping at picture-perfect Primošten. Watch the superyachts go by as you enjoy a pizza on Trogir's Riva, and explore the Unesco-protected old town. Then head past Split airport to join your skippered yacht in Marina Kaštela, dining in a rustic *konoba* nearby.

Day 2 — Opatija

En route to Opatija, take a detour to explore the medieval hilltop town of Motovun and sample the local truffles. In Opatija, admire the grand villas along the seafront and enjoy coffee and cream cake at a Viennese-era café.

OF CROATIA

Day 7 · Korčula

Sail to Korčula town and spend the day in one of Croatia's most stunning medieval cities. Pick up some fresh fish and local delicacies for dinner on board the next day. While in town, dine in style and enjoy the incredible views at LD on the terrace of the Lešić-Dimitri Palace (see page 140).

Day 9 · Dubrovnik

Disembark in Dubrovnik and walk the city walls before getting a taxi to the airport. If you have time, go first to nearby Cavtat and take a diving trip to discover some of Croatia's many Greek and Roman relics, or simply relax over a late lunch at one of the city's seafront restaurants.

Day 6 · Hvar

Cast off and take a peek at Diocletian's Palace from Split's bay, before making for a deserted anchorage on the Pakleni islands, near Hvar. Take an afternoon swim before heading off to Hvar town for an evening exploring its nightlife and history.

Day 8 · Mljet

Take your time sailing between the Pelješac peninsula and Mljet island, perhaps stopping off for a swim in Mljet's salt-water lakes. Anchor off the northeast coast of Lokrum island to watch the city lights of Dubrovnik while feasting on fresh fish on board.

CONTENTS

Introduction 9

A Brief History 15

Where to Go 27
❶ *Numbered map references pinpoint the sights*

Zagreb. 27
Donji Grad 28, Trg Bana Josip Jelačića 30, Kaptol 30, Gornji Grad 31, Novi Zagreb 34, Parks and Gardens 34

Inland Croatia 35
North of Zagreb 35, Plitvice Lakes 37, Slavonia 38

Istria 41
Pula 42, Vodnjan 44, Rovinj 44, Poreč 46, Other Coastal Resorts 48, Boat Trips from the Coastal Resorts 49, Istrian Interior 50

Kvarner Gulf 52
Rijeka 53, The Opatija Riviera 54, Paklenica National Park 56, Kvarner Gulf Islands 56

Dalmatia 59
Northern Dalmatia 60, Southern Dalmatia: Split 66, South of Split 69, Dubrovnik 70, Dalmatian Islands 76

What to Do............ 83

Sports........................ 83

Shopping..................... 87

Entertainment................. 92

Croatia for Children............. 94

Eating Out............. 96

A–Z Travel Tips........... 111

Recommended Hotels...... 133

Index...................... 142

Features

Blue Flag Beaches and Marinas........... 10

The Siege of Dubrovnik................. 23

Historic Landmarks.................... 25

Mirogoj Cemetery.................... 35

Jasenovac Camp...................... 40

James Joyce......................... 43

Istrian Wines........................ 47

Hiking Opportunities................. 57

Dolphins of Lošinj.................... 59

Truffles........................... 88

Calendar of Events................... 95

Restaurant Culture................... 105

INTRODUCTION

Croatia may be one of Europe's newest nations, gaining its independence in a bloody divorce from Yugoslavia in 1991, but it is already one of the world's most alluring tourist destinations. A member of the European Union since 2013, Croatia's small size is deceptive, at just 56,594 sq km (21,845 sq miles). An incredible variety of scenery is packed into this boomerang-shaped country, from the magnificent 1,778km (1,105 mile) -long coastline, to the lofty mountains and sweeping fertile plains of the interior. Croatia's identity has been shaped by its position at a political and ethnic crossroads, across the Adriatic from Italy, and bordered by Slovenia, Hungary, Serbia, Bosnia-Herzegovina and Montenegro.

A Natural Playground

Croatia's most dramatic natural attraction is its Adriatic coastline, which sweeps from Slovenia in the north to the Montenegrin border in the south, taking in 1,246 islands, islets and reefs en route. Crystal-clear water and countless bays and coves lure visitors and locals alike. In summer the climate is glorious, with hot sunny days tempered by a cooling sea breeze. Even in the spring and autumn the mercury usually rises high enough to allow T-shirts to be worn.

Away from the beaches, massive mountain ranges offer opportunities for hiking,

Unesco sites

Unesco has listed seven World Heritage Sites in Croatia: Dubrovnik and Trogir old towns, Diocletian's Palace and medieval Split, the Plitvice Lakes, the Euphrasian Basilica in Poreč, Šibenik Cathedral and Stari Grad Plain on Hvar island.

Looking out over the Kornati Islands

climbing and extreme sports. Further inland there is the Unesco World Heritage Site of Plitvice Lakes National Park, a limestone oasis of gushing streams, pounding waterfalls and green-hued lakes. Perhaps less visited by tourists, but in its own way just as impressive is the Krka National Park in Dalmatia, with a series of lakes and streams plunging inexorably towards the Adriatic in a dramatic passage through the karst backbone of the country.

Croatia's varied landscape also makes it a Mecca for sports enthusiasts. It is a popular destination for sailing, as recognised by billionaires such as Bill Gates, who bring their yachts to cruise around the islands. This breed of luxury traveller is catered for by an increasing number of chic restaurants and hotels that are a far cry from the faceless concrete blocks that kicked off Croatian tourism in the 1960s.

The sailors flocking to the 55 marinas that dot the coastline are being joined by scuba divers. Conditions are excellent for diving, with a range of sites suitable for divers of all levels. The island of Biševo with its famous Blue Grotto is every bit as alluring as its Italian counterpart in Capri, and around the neighbouring island of Vis there are at least a dozen shipwrecks suitable for diving. All along the coast there are diving schools where novices can make their first dive and the more

Blue Flag Beaches and Marinas

Croatia may not have many of the fine sandy beaches that you find in Italy and Spain, but it does have some of the cleanest beaches anywhere in Europe. There are more than 100 Blue Flag beaches and nearly 20 Blue Flag marinas dotted along the coastline. The Blue Flag is awarded by the European Union in recognition of cleanliness, something that the authorities are keen to ensure through their conservation programmes. For a full list of Croatia's Blue Flag beaches and marinas, see www.blueflag.org.

The falls at Skradinski Buk, Krka National Park

experienced can organise explorations of one of the least spoilt diving destinations in Europe.

Cities and Towns

While Croatia has eight national parks, its towns and cities also hold plenty of interest. Zagreb, the capital and most populous city, is a large, modern metropolis complete with high-class hotels, richly stocked museums and restaurants that reflect its cosmopolitan nature. To the south, the Austrian-Hungarian architectural and political influences of Zagreb and Varaždin give way on the coast to Venetian and Roman remnants.

Split, Croatia's second-largest city, is a chaotic, sprawling centre built on the shores of the Adriatic with its core housed inside the 2,000-year-old Diocletian's Palace. This World Heritage city-within-a-city is bursting with bars, cafés and boutiques that are all wrapped up in a Mediterranean buzz.

Croatia's depth of history comes from centuries of conflict in which the Greeks, Romans, French, Venetians and Hungarians have all vied for control. The legacy of this eclectic past is evident in world-class attractions such as the 2,000-year-old Roman Arena in Pula and the mosaic-embellished Basilica of Euphrasius in Poreč, another World Heritage site. It also surfaces when you least expect it, when a Venetian bell tower emerges above an insignificant town or when you come upon an arrow-straight thoroughfare that has been smoothed over by Roman sandals.

Croatia also has its own home-grown architectural highlights such as Šibenik and, the most striking town of them all, Dubrovnik. Nicknamed the 'Pearl of the Adriatic' by Byron, this stunning city-state has been immaculately preserved in its original Baroque glory. Walking around Dubrovnik during the renowned summer festival and savouring the sun melting

Dubrovnik, one of the most beautiful cities in Europe

into the Adriatic from the city's ramparts are unforgettable experiences.

A Split Personality

The locals of Zagreb and Split live very different lives that hint at the contrast between the two main cultures in Croatia: the Central

Holy folk

Religion in Croatia follows ethnic lines and the Croat majority are predominantly Roman Catholic, with the country receiving four papal visits since independence. Minority religions include Serbian Orthodox and Islam.

European order and rationality of the north and the more laid-back lifestyle of the coast, where the steamy summer days slow things down. In the capital they talk of their coastal brethren as being lazy, while in Split, where people pride themselves on their chic sense of style and sophistication, Zagreb is dismissed as being dull and uptight. It is a rivalry that ripples through the nation. Bring the Serbs of Krajina, the Bosnians of the border areas and the Slovenian influences of the northwest into the mix and more contrasting lifestyles emerge, with the varying ways of life coexisting today in relative harmony.

The legacy of the War

Despite what the national tourist office may hope, it is difficult to write about Croatia without mentioning 'the war'. Images of a burning Dubrovnik and helpless refugees filled TV screens across the world in the early 1990s. However, the reality is that, except in a few places such as Vukovar and Knin, it is hard to tell that the bitter conflict ever burned through the country. Indeed, it is perhaps the years of communism combined with the Homeland War that have kept Dubrovnik, its riviera and Croatia's other treasures unspoilt for so long. It is only when you make a conscious effort to search for clues that the scars emerge, such as differently coloured roof tiles and deserted villages of burnt-out houses. For

Croatian football fans

those interested in what happened, many locals are only too keen to talk to anyone showing an interest in a conflict that some Croats still feel the rest of Europe did not do enough to prevent or to bring to an end.

Croatia Today

Croatia has made rapid progress in putting itself on the map since independence, not least with international sporting successes (see page 24). Tourism is expanding rapidly as tour operators of all sizes are rushing to offer everything from villa and beach holidays to sailing, hiking and other adventure tours. This has been helped by the speedy growth of budget air-travel routes and the expansion of the national motorway network.

Croatia's post-war progress was partially put on hold by the controversial right-wing president Franjo Tudman, but after his death in 1999 the country was welcomed into the global fold. In July 2013, Croatia became a member of the European Union, showing the country's dramatic rise from a war-torn corner of Yugoslavia into a modern European nation. The country was affected by the economic downturn following the financial crisis of 2007–2008, although not to the extent of some of its more venerable EU neighbours. Croatia remains one of Europe's most beautiful and alluring tourist destinations.

A BRIEF HISTORY

Delving into the complex history of one of Europe's youngest nations throws up as many unresolved questions as answers. Croatia has been an independent nation on only three occasions: during the reign of the Croatian kings in the 10th and 11th centuries, during World War II, though it was essentially a Nazi puppet state, and since 1991 after its bitter separation from Yugoslavia. Most Croats today have always felt a strong sense of national identity despite previously being labelled as Yugoslav on their passports. All this makes gleaning unbiased historical information from within the country a tricky task.

From Prehistory

Thanks to the discovery of 'Krapina Man' and his Neanderthal kinsmen in the Zagorje region (see page 35) in the 19th century, it has been possible to trace habitation in Croatia to 30,000BC. The hilltop settlement where the remains were found, near the small town of Krapina, is one of the most important prehistoric sites in Europe. Along the Croatian coast there is also a scattering of evidence that hunter-gatherers may have settled in the region at least 20,000 years ago.

Greeks, Romans and Byzantines

By the time the Greeks arrived on the island of Vis in the 4th century BC, a smattering of tribes known as the Illyrians inhabited both the coastal areas and hinterland. From 229BC onwards the Romans moved into the region, rapidly swallowing up large chunks

Emperor Diocletian

The Roman emperor Diocletian was probably born in Salona (near Split). Upon retirement in around AD300, he returned to his roots and built a vast palace, which still stands today.

of the country and beginning their makeover by building solid roads and structured towns, and imposing their way of life. The amphitheatre in Pula (see page 42) dates from this period, as does Diocletian's Palace in Split (see page 66). Many other reminders of Roman heritage can be seen in Croatia today.

The Romans continued to hold sway over the region until the western part of their empire collapsed in the 5th century. For a short time Croatia was ruled by the Ostrogoths, before the eastern part of the Roman Empire, known as Byzantium, gained control of Istria and Dalmatia. The dominance of the first few centuries of Roman rule never truly returned, with persistent threats both from the Illyrians and the Asian Avars.

Croatia's Kings

The Croats are widely thought to be a Slavic people who came to the region in a mass migration from the plains to the north. Their Slavic cousins, the Serbs and Slovenes, are also thought to have moved to the area around this time. As more Croats arrived, their influence grew and they acquired their own king, Tomislav, a heroic character still revered in Croatia. In securing the Croatian state in 925, Tomislav saw off both the Venetian Republic and the Hungarians. Following the end of Tomislav's reign in 928, a succession of kings took their turn as the Croatian monarch, but Tomislav remains the symbolic hero.

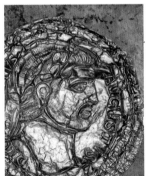

Diocletian with a laurel wreath

It was during this period that Croats began converting to Christianity. Recognition by the Pope in the 9th century marked their allegiance to the Roman rather than the

Remnants of the Glagolitic alphabet in Hum, Istria

Byzantine Church. Grgur (Gregory) of Nin, a Slav bishop, tried to establish a Croatian national church, championing the use of an alphabet called Glagolitic and the performance of Mass in the vernacular. However, the Latin clergy defeated his attempts.

Coveted by Hungary and Venice

An agreement in 1102 confirmed Hungarian control over most of Croatia, although the Croats were allowed a degree of autonomy and their own representative (*ban*) and parliament (*sabor*). The Hungarian involvement in Croatia continued for many centuries. In the first three they faced persistent threats from the Ottoman Empire to the east. The fear of the Islamic 'hordes' underpinned the way Budapest viewed Croatia. Across the country's rugged interior a series of fortifications (*krajina*) were spread out as a bulwark against the Ottomans, a barrier that was ultimately successful, but often teetered on the verge of being overrun.

As Hungary secured much of inland Croatia, the Venetians moved in to snatch swathes of coastline, over which they took control in 1420. Dubrovnik was one of the few places to retain its independence. The Venetians, like the Romans centuries earlier, brought in their own architectural ideas and town plans, leaving an indelible impression on the Croatian coast that lingers to this day in fortified towns, fine buildings and elegant church bell towers. The Venetian hold was always tenuous, based more on securing trade routes than acquiring and governing territory, and they faced persistent threats not only from the Ottomans but also from pirates such as the infamous marauders of Senj.

The Fall of the Divine Republic

As the 18th century came to a close, the French, under Napoleon, finally triggered the end of the Venetian Republic in 1797. Among the booty they collected were the Venetian possessions along the Croatian coast. The history of Napoleon's 'Illyrian Provinces' was to be short-lived after the French defeat at the hands of Russia in the winter of 1812–13. The Austro-Hungarians were on hand to pick up the pieces and the Treaty of Vienna confirmed their gains in 1815.

Despite, or perhaps because of, spending centuries under the will of various powers, Croatian identity and patriotism started to reassert itself in the first half of the 19th century. The result was that Josip Jelačić, a popular army officer from the Vojna Krajina, became *ban* (governor) of Croatia, though he was careful to pledge loyalty to the Habsburg Empire. This drive for recognition manifested itself most strongly in the cultural and linguistic fields, and it came at a time of similar Serb and Slovene risings in what evolved into a pan-Slavism movement.

World Wars I and II

The dissolution of the Austro-Hungarian Empire that was precipitated by World War I presented an ideal opportunity for this pan-Slavism to become something more solid, with the formation of the Kingdom of the Serbs, Croats and Slovenes in 1918 (known as Yugoslavia after 1930). Despite high hopes and official talk of unity, many Croats were disappointed to find that, instead of the loose federalism they had anticipated, much of the real power shifted to Belgrade.

When Germany swept into Croatia in April 1941, extremist members of the Ustaše Party, under Ante Pavelić, seized the opportunity and collaborated in the setting up of a Nazi puppet state. The war brought out the worst in some Croats, and Pavelić and his cronies established a concentration camp at Jasenovac where Serbs, Jews and other 'undesirables' were murdered (see page 40). This sorry chapter in Croatia's history ended in 1945 with Tito's communist partisans taking control of Yugoslavia and massacring thousands of Ustaše forces and collaborators.

Dubrovnik was once an independent republic called Ragusa

Croatia under Tito

Tito (born Josip Broz, 1892–1980), himself a Croat, kept a tight rein over Yugoslavia during his four decades as president and Communist Party leader. Croatian nationalism was suppressed, as were nationalist sentiments in Bosnia, Serbia and Kosovo, though they still simmered below the surface. Economic resentment grew in Croatia from the 1960s when mass tourism started bringing in substantial amounts of hard currency, which was often siphoned away from the coast to swell central government coffers in Belgrade.

The disenchantment helped to fuel desires for greater self-government, which manifested itself in the Croatian Spring. This involved reform-minded politicians and intellectuals, some of whom called for Croatian to be recognised as a separate language from Serbian. The Croatian League of Communists was split between those who wanted to keep the status quo

Tito as a young partisan during World War II

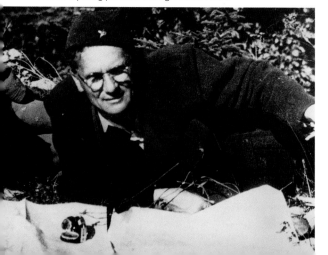

and those looking for greater autonomy, a tension that was expressed in student riots in the early 1970s. Seeing the unity of Yugoslavia threatened, Tito moved in to clamp down on the Croatian Spring, with sackings and forced resignations in December 1971.

Ethnic Rivalries and the Descent to War

While Tito had been largely successful in suppressing the worst of the ethnic rivalries

Slovenia escapes

Slovenia declared independence from Yugoslavia on the same day as Croatia – 25 June 1991. However, with far fewer ethnic Serbs among its population and with no history of ethnic cleansing, it did not provoke the savage reaction from Serbia that Croatia drew. After a brief skirmish with the Slovenes, the Yugoslav Army evacuated Slovenia with barely a murmur.

within Yugoslavia, he had been less successful in grooming an heir. His death in 1980 created a power vacuum and a sense of instability that ultimately paved the way for the bloody Balkan wars of the 1990s. In the absence of Tito, the Yugoslav presidency was left to a rotating collective, representing the republics.

Amid political wrangling and machinations, the then little-known Serbian politician Slobodan Milošević emerged to assert Serbian nationalism and endorse the view that Belgrade was not interested in letting the various parts of Yugoslavia enjoy an amicable separation. As moves towards independence took hold in Slovenia and Croatia, many Serbs, including Milošević, realised that dissolution was inevitable and instigated a plan that involved setting up a 'Greater Serbia' by swallowing large sections of the other parts of Yugoslavia.

Tensions finally reached a head in June 1991 when Slovenia and Croatia declared their independence. An ex-Yugoslav general, Franjo Tuđman, was at the helm of a new Croatian nation, which was not officially recognised by the United Nations and which faced the immediate danger of the Serbs

Dubrovnik under siege in 1991

within its borders combining with the powerful Yugoslav Army to cut off parts of its territory and claim them for 'Greater Serbia'.

The Homeland War

From June 1991 onwards, the fighting escalated rapidly as the rebel Serbs and the Yugoslav National Army (jna) used their military superiority against the poorly armed Croatian police and guard units to 'ethnically cleanse' swathes of Croatia. Milošević gambled on a quick victory before the international community became involved, but the rapid Serb successes in central Croatia were halted in Slavonia by the defiant stand of the people of the eastern city of Vukovar. This city stood on the border with Serbia and bore the brunt of heavy shelling and air raids as it became cut off and a siege of medieval ferocity ensued. Vukovar's resistance was echoed in the south by Dubrovnik, which was also besieged. Both cities became patriotic symbols of Croatian resistance.

Although Vukovar did eventually fall and Serbian forces committed further atrocities to those that had already scarred their military advances around the country, Zagreb was never threatened. Serb military progress soon slowed as the Croats managed to gather hardware and personnel together for a more organised defence. In the spring of 1992, soon after Germany had unilaterally recognised Croatian independence, UN units were deployed as a buffer between the two sides following international negotiations.

The peace deal froze the battle lines and promised to return territory to the Croatians, but the vague timescale did not satisfy Tuđman. His government continued to acquire military equipment in a period when the rebel Serbs had lost the backing of the Yugoslav Army. In 1995, the Croatian 'Flash' (May) and 'Storm' (August) offensives may have incited the ire of the UN, but the Croats rapidly regained much rebel Serb territory. In 1998, as part of the Erdut agreement, the last tracts of Slavonia, including devastated Vukovar, were handed back to Croatia and the Homeland War was at an end.

With the establishment of the International War Crimes Tribunal for the former Yugoslavia at The Hague, various notable indictees, most recently Radovan Karadžić, have gradually been brought to trial, though two prime culprits, Tuđman and Milošević, both died before being sentenced. Charges of war crimes against Croatian forces and national heroes provoked fury among many Croats, but the country did make made steps to co-operate with the tribunal, with the arrest of

The Siege of Dubrovnik

The siege of Dubrovnik was only the most publicised of a series of attacks from the Yugoslav Army, but it was the one that made headline news around the world. The city had no particular strategic value nor any real Serb claim of ownership (the Serb population was around 7 percent), but it was surrounded by a naval blockade and shelled from the surrounding hills for seven months, its 50,000 inhabitants trapped behind the medieval city walls. Electricity and communications were cut and the citizens found themselves sheltering in candlelit basements; even the yachts in the harbour were blown up. By the end of the siege, more than 500 historic buildings had been damaged and 43 citizens killed.

General Ante Gotovina in Spain in 2005. Sentenced to prison in 2011, he was acquitted by appeal in 2012.

Croatia Today

As one of Europe's newest nations Croatia has quickly established itself on the world stage, not least in its sporting achievements since the millennium. Goran Ivanišević became the first wildcard entry to win Wimbledon in 2001 and the national tennis team became the first unseeded winners of the Davis Cup in 2005. In 2002 Janica Kostelić won Croatia's first three Olympic gold medals in skiing and a gold and silver in Turin in 2006. Her brother, Ivica, won two silvers at the 2010 Toronto Games. The Croatians were runners-up in the World Men's Handball Championship of 2009.

Croatia's emergence on the political and economic stage has been slower, in part because in the early years the right-wing policies and abrasive style of President Franjo Tuđman marred the country's image abroad. Since his death in 1999, Croatia has been welcomed back into the international community and foreign investment has grown. The government demonstrated its determination to enhance Croatia's profile by its improved co-operation with the War Crimes Tribunal at The Hague.

Folk-dancing to celebrate Croatia's accession to the EU

The country was still plagued by corruption, however, and the imprisonment of former prime minister Ivo Sanader in 2012 was a low point. But Croatia's concerted efforts to clean itself up were rewarded with long-awaited EU membership in 2013.

Historic Landmarks

30,000BC 'Krapina Man' evidence of prehistoric settlement in Croatia.

1000BC Illyrian tribes begin living in the region.

229BC–AD600 Roman then Byzantine empires hold sway.

600–700 Arrival of Slavic tribes from north of the Danube.

925 King Tomislav becomes the first king of an independent Croatia.

1102 Hungarian control over Croatia agreed.

1420s Venetian Republic occupies much of the Croatian coast.

1797 Venetian Republic collapses to Napoleon.

1918 Kingdom of Serbs, Croats and Slovenes proclaimed.

1929 Fascist Ustaše set-up under Ante Pavelić.

1941 German troops invade and Ustaše collaborates in establishing the Independent State of Croatia (ndh).

May 1945 Tito's Partisans enter Zagreb, marking the start of Communist rule. Tito is declared prime minister of the new Yugoslav Federal Republic.

1960s Croatian Spring marks a desire for independence.

1980 Death of Tito leaves power vacuum.

1990 Moves towards Croatian independence led by Franjo Tuđman.

25 June 1991 Declaration of independence; Croatian Serbs revolt with the backing of the Yugoslav military. The Homeland War breaks out.

18 November 1991 Fall of Vukovar marks nadir of the war.

January 1992 United Nations brokers a ceasefire.

1995 Croatian 'Flash' (May) and 'Storm' (August) offensives regain much of rebel Serb territory.

1998 Last occupied areas returned to Croatia through the UN.

1999 Death of President Tuđman.

2005 The opening of serious negotiations for EU membership.

2009 Croatia joins Nato.

2010 Croatia has three new additions to Unesco's List of Intangible Cultural Heritage in Need of Urgent Safeguarding, including Ojkanje, a bizarre voice-shaking style of singing.

2013 Croatia joins the European Union.

WHERE TO GO

Most of Croatia's tourist industry is concentrated on the Adriatic coast, in Dalmatia and the Istrian peninsula, including the numerous islands. International airports serving the coast include Dubrovnik, Split, Zadar, Rijeka and Pula. A motorway system (www.hac.hr) connects most of the country's main cities and runs along the coastline to Ploče near Korčula. This is a big improvement on the scenic but often slow and serpentine coastal road, the Jadranska Magistrala (Adriatic Highway). Island-hopping is a great way to experience coastal Croatia; the main ferry company is Jadrolinija, www.jadrolinija.hr.

Inland Croatia also has plenty to interest visitors, including the lively capital Zagreb, impressive mountain scenery, castles, spas and the outstanding Plitvice Lakes National Park. From Zagreb, the *autocesta* (motorway) runs east to Slavonia.

ZAGREB

A charming old quarter, a number of museums and leafy parks and a lively nightlife make **Zagreb ❶** an ideal city-break destination. Many people heading for the coast tend to bypass the capital and

Zagreb Card

The Zagreb Card represents good value if you plan to spend some time in the city. Choose from 24 or 72 hours. Holders are entitled to reductions in admission charges to most galleries and museums and free public transport, as well as theatre, restaurant and nightclub discounts. The card is available from the tourist information office on Trg Bana Josip Jelačića, most Zagreb hotels, or see www. zagrebcard.fivestars.hr.

Zagreb Cathedral

in doing so miss out on this compact, lively metropolis, whose younger residents give it a buzz that is particularly evident in its myriad cafés on a balmy evening. Be aware, however, that the city dwellers too tend to head for the coast in the summer months, during which time the hot capital becomes abnormally quiet.

Donji Grad

Spreading north of Glavni Kolodvor, the central railway station, is Donji Grad (Lower Town). Standing proud in Trg Kralja Tomislava, the square opposite the station, is the equestrian **statue of King Tomislav Ⓐ**, the first of the Croatian kings, his commanding figure a symbol of the city and meeting point.

North of the central railway station is a string of neatly tended squares, often filled with students reclining on benches and older citizens idling by the fountains. Trg Kralja Tomislava is home to the **Art Pavilion** (Umjetnički Paviljon; www.umjetnicki-paviljon.hr; Tue–Sat 11am–7pm, Sun 10am–1pm; charge), an Art Nouveau building housing temporary exhibitions.

The next park north is Strossmayer Trg, containing the **Strossmayer Gallery Ⓑ** (Strossmayerova Galerija; Tue 10am–1pm and 5–7pm, Wed–Sun 10am–1pm; charge). It was commissioned by the eponymous Slavonian bishop in the 19th century and has a collection of works by Italian masters including Tintoretto and Veronese. Look out also for the Baška Tablet, said to be the oldest example of Croatian Glagolitic script, brought here from its original home on the Kvarner Gulf island of Krk.

A few blocks west, in Trg Maršala Tita, is the **Museum Of Arts and Crafts Ⓒ** (Muzej za Umjetnost i Obrt; www.muo. hr; Tue–Sat 10am–7pm, Sun 10am–2pm; charge), designed by the Austrian architect Hermann Bollé, whose name pops up all over the city, including the Mirogoj Cemetery (see page 35). The eclectic collection includes ceramics and furniture, clocks, silverware, glass and religious art. Next-door is the grand, neo-Baroque architecture of the Croatian National Theatre.

Diagonally opposite the museum, facing Rooseveltov Trg, is Zagreb's most impressive museum; the **Mimara** Ⓓ (Muzej Mimara; Tue–Sat 10am–5pm, open until 7pm Thur, Sun 10am–2pm; charge), housed in an old grammar school. The artists represented include Raphael, Caravaggio, Rembrandt, Rubens, Van Dyck, Velázquez, Gainsborough, Turner, Delacroix, Renoir, Manet and Degas. There have been persistent mutterings from certain sections of the art world about the dubious authenticity of some of the work, but if you take it on face value the 4,000-strong collection is impressive. The contents were donated to the city by Dalmatian collector

The Art Pavilion

Ante Topić Mimara and also include archaeological finds from around the Mediterranean.

Trg Bana Josip Jelačića

The epicentre of Zagreb life, **Trg Bana Josip Jelačića E**, is surrounded by grand 19th-century buildings. The statue of the viceroy, Ban Josip Jelačić, erected in 1866 and banished by Tito in 1945, has been returned to its prominent position at the heart of this plaza. Today, the square is the best place to take the pulse of the city.

Kaptol

The Kaptol district breaks away uphill from Trg Bana Josip Jelačića. Without doubt, the highlight here is the neo-Gothic **Zagreb Cathedral F** (opening times vary; free) with its twin bell towers, designed by Hermann Bollé. A religious building

Trg Bana Josip Jelačića sets the pace of the city

has stood on the site since the reign of the Croatian kings in the 10th century and it is still a place of devotion for many local residents. Notable features include a series of 13th-century frescoes that have survived the cathedral's numerous traumas, including a devastating earthquake in the 19th century. The cathedral is also the last resting place of the controversial Croatian clergyman Archbishop Stepinac (d.1960), who was accused of

Angel on Zagreb Cathedral

colluding with the Nazi puppet regime during World War II, but is considered a martyr by many Croats. Look out for Ivan Meštrović's relief of Christ with Stepinac.

A short walk west from the cathedral is **Dolac Market**, where locals can be seen haggling over the fresh fruit, flowers and vegetables. A sprinkling of bars and restaurants overlook the small market square, providing a good view of the action. If you're planning on catching a train from Zagreb to Budapest, Vienna or the coast, the market is a good place to stock up on provisions, if you get there before 1pm.

Gornji Grad

The oldest part of the city is Gornji Grad (Upper Town), which still retains some of its historical charm. You can reach it by walking up from the cathedral, but it is more fun to take the funicular from Donji Grad. At the top is the **Lotrščak Tower G** (Kula Lotrščak; daily 9am–9pm; charge), where an art gallery with a modest array of paintings for sale is a prelude to the main attraction – a sweeping view of the city from the observation level, accompanied at noon by loud cannon blasts.

Just north of the tower is one of Zagreb's most intriguing attractions, the **Museum of Broken Relationships** (Muzeij prekinutih veza; www.brokenships.com; summer open daily 9am–10.30pm, winter 9am–9pm; charge). Stories of love lost and found are told through objects donated by people around the world, and the result is poignant and compelling.

Below Lotrščak Tower, **Strossmayer Parade** (Strossmayerovo šetalište) offers similarly fine views of the city spreading across the plain, with its main buildings, including the cathedral, clearly visible. The most intriguing bench from which to savour the vista is the work of modern artist Ivan Kožarić, with the bronze figure of the writer Antun Gustav Matoš awaiting someone to share the view with him.

St Mark's Church roof detail

A short walk north brings you to **St Mark's Church** (opening times vary; free). This striking church features a multi-coloured 19th-century roof, upon which the Croatian coat of arms is clearly visible. The church itself dates back to the 13th century, though there have been many major renovations over the centuries. Inside are several works by Ivan Meštrović, including

Dolac Market

a sinewy depiction of Christ on the cross in typically challenging Meštrović style.

Fans of the 20th-century cult Croatian sculptor will not want to miss the **Meštrović Atelier** (Tue–Fri 10am–6pm, Sat–Sun 10am–2pm; charge), just north of St Mark's. Meštrović lived here from 1924 to 1942 and the displays of his original sketches and plans illuminate many of the works that can be seen around Zagreb, including the *Crucifixion* in St Mark's Church and the statue of *Grgur of Nin*, outside Diocletian's Palace in Split, with a replica in Varaždin.

Further north, the **Zagreb City Museum** (Muzej Grada Zagreba; Muzej grada Zagreba; www.mgz.hr; Tue–Fri 10am–6pm, Sat 11am–7pm, Sun 10am–2pm; charge, free guided tour Sat and Sun 11am) features, among other displays, scale models that help visitors to understand the different phases of the city from medieval times to the modern day.

In the shadow of Gornji Grad is **Tkalčićeva** . This cobbled thoroughfare is lined with pavement cafés and on busy nights it is packed with people out to see and be seen. There are so many cafés to choose from, the best option is to stroll along its length a couple of times before you settle down

Mirogoj Cemetery

and order your coffee or an Ožujsko, the excellent locally brewed lager.

Novi Zagreb

South of the Sava river, the urban post-war sprawl is brightened by Zagreb's **National Library**, **Lisinski Concert Hall** and, most impressively, by the **Museum of Contemporary Art** (Muzej Suvremene Umjetnosti; www.msu.hr; Tue–Sun 11am–6pm, Sat 11am–8pm; charge). This enormous space contains more than 4,000 works by 900 artists, including a large film and video collection.

Parks and Gardens

Zagreb's green spaces provide a welcome escape from the bustle of city life on a hot day. West of the station are the **Botanical Gardens** (Botanički Vrt; Apr–Oct Mon–Tue 9am–2.30pm, Wed–Sun 9am–7pm (6pm in early spring and late autumn); free), established at the end of the 19th century. About 10,000 species are packed into small confines, surrounded by paths and benches, and one of the pools is home to carp and a colony of terrapins.

Maksimir Park is only a short tram ride 3km (1.86 miles) east of the city centre and spreads out across 128 hectares (316 acres). Both the national football team and local side Dinamo Zagreb play their home games at the crumbling sports stadium facing the park. The atmosphere during games can be rowdy, but there is no better venue to see both Croatian patriotism and the local citizens' love of Zagreb expressed so vehemently. Within the park boundaries are **Zagreb Zoo** (9am–sunset; charge), a boating lake and walkways, as well as plenty of shady trees.

Lake Jarun is also only a short tram ride from the city centre, 4km (2.48 miles) to the southwest. As well as an artificial lake, there are cafés, restaurants and bars that are open day and night in summer.

INLAND CROATIA

North of Zagreb

Varaždin ❷ is the only city in the **Zagorje** region, which extends north of Zagreb towards Hungary and Slovenia. The

Mirogoj Cemetery

The Mirogoj Cemetery (free) is the place to be if you are dead in Zagreb. Here, in one of Europe's grandest graveyards, the city's richest residents and luminaries vie for space.

A local joke makes fun of the fact that many of the deceased inhabitants of Mirogoj have far more impressive abodes than the living citizens of the city, and there is more than a little truth to this. The cemetery was built in 1876, the majority of it the work of Hermann Bollé, whose extravagant tastes and designs are evident both here and elsewhere in the city. The entrance is particularly striking: an elegant neoclassical façade draped in ivy with a colonnade and a row of four lime green cupolas topped off with one large central dome.

It is worth spending some time admiring the sculptures and grand tombs that grace the interior. Look out too for the memorial to the victims of the Homeland War, with a monument inscribed with the names of 13,500 dead, situated just outside the main gate.

There are regular buses from the cathedral to Mirogoj Cemetery.

Varaždin's castle

Zagorje is a hilly green playground for the citizens of Zagreb, who come to visit the chocolate-box castles, relax in the spas and sample the local food and drink. A good sweep of the Zagorje can be covered in a long day trip from Zagreb, but to get a real feel for this rewarding region it's worth basing yourself in Varaždin for a few days.

Varaždin's old town, which is more than 800 years old and for a brief period was Croatia's capital city, is being smartened up. There are also ambitions to have the city's main tourist attraction, its stunning **castle**, put on Unesco's World Heritage list. The fortifications date back to the 12th century, and in the 16th century the castle was an integral part of an attempt by the Austrian-Hungarians to fend off the attentions of the Ottoman Empire. When the threat of Ottoman invasion ceased, the local Erdödy family bought the fortress and transformed it into a grand home. Today, it houses the **City Museum** (Gradski Muzej Varaždin; www.gmv.hr; Tue–Fri 9am–5pm, Sat–Sun 9am–1pm; charge).

Varaždin's Fortress is one of a string of castles that are spread out over the Zagorje, set amid the rolling hills and forests that characterise the landscape. One of the most appealing is **Trakošćan Castle** (www.trakoscan.hr; Apr–Sept 9am–6pm, Oct–Mar 9am–4pm; charge), less than an hour's drive west of Varaždin, and another popular excursion from the capital. A castle has stood on the site since the 16th century, but the one that is open to the public today is largely the result of a rather fanciful 19th-century remoulding. The castle is worth a few hours' exploration, as are the surrounding grounds where a small lake has a path running around its shores and a café by the water's edge. Also on the Unesco tentative list is **Veliki Tabor** (www.veliki-tabor.hr; Tue–Fri 9am–5pm, until 4pm in winter, Sat–Sun 9am–7pm, until 5pm in winter; charge), a ruggedly impressive castle dating back to the 12th century.

The Zagorje gained a reputation as a spa retreat in the 19th century when visitors from Austria would come to take the waters. Of the spas left today, **Krapinske Toplice** (charge) is one of the best. There are a number of pools of varying temperature, from lukewarm to steaming hot, where you can join in the relaxed fun.

Trakošćan Castle

Plitvice Lakes

The **Plitvice Lakes National Park** ❸ (NP Plitvička Jezera; www.np-plitvicka-jezera.hr; charge), 110km (68 miles) south of Zagreb on the old road to Split, is one of Croatia's top attractions and was added to Unesco's World Heritage list in 1979.

Whatever the season, the beauty of Plitvice is immediately evident. The fresh, clear waters rush through a network of 16 lakes and tumble down waterfalls stretching for some 8km (5 miles). You can visit the lakes on a day trip from Zagreb or from the southern cities and resorts, but it is best to spend a night at one of the state-owned hotels inside the park boundaries. Wildlife within the park includes otter and deer, wild boar and even bears, not to mention a wide variety of fish and birds.

Getting around Plitvice could not be easier, as the trails and wooden walkways are connected by electric boats and tourist trains. Hopping on and off the boats and traversing the wooden walkways as the spray of the waterfalls mists all around is part of the fun.

In high season don't be deterred by the crowds: set off early in the morning and head south to Lake Proščansko, which is usually quiet and peaceful all year round. Often the best plan is to divide your visit into at least two adventures: one to the remote upper lakes and another to the more popular lower lakes, avoiding the temptation to cover everything too quickly. Swimming in the lakes is prohibited.

Slavonia

The often neglected eastern region of Slavonia has plenty to offer, not least the fact that it is never overrun with tourists. As in Zagreb, though, you may find most of the population has escaped to the coast in July and August. It is just a 3-hour drive east along the *autocesta* (motorway) from Zagreb.

Plitvice Lakes National Park

The city of **Osijek** ❹ is a good base for exploring the area and sampling the excellent wines, with a growing number of wine tours and cellars to visit. It's also close to **Kopački rit Nature Park** (www.kopacki-rit.com; charge), one of the biggest areas of remaining wetland in Europe, providing a broad range of tours and activities. However, 35km (22 miles) along the trunk road from the *autocesta* to Osijek it is worth stopping off at the small town of **Đakovo** to visit its stunning cathedral, whose lofty twin towers can be seen from afar. The neo-Gothic cathedral, built between 1862 and 1882, was commissioned by the Croatian clergyman Bishop Strossmayer. A sculpture of

Strossmayer sits gazing back towards the monumental building from across the road. Đakovo also has a Lippizaner horse stud farm (www.ergela-djakovo.hr) with a history that can be traced back to the 13th century.

Osijek was subject to savage Serb attacks during the Homeland War, but the city has since regained its verve, helped by a young student population and a lively café scene along the River Drava. The core of the city is blessed with some impressive architecture, most notably on Europska Avenija, which has a collage of Art Nouveau buildings. Bishop Strossmayer commissioned the massive Cathedral of St Peter and St Paul, built in neo-Gothic style at the end of the 19th century.

A 10-minute stroll from Europska is **Tvrđa**. This old quarter was neglected for decades and the Serbs shelled it heavily in the early 1990s, but efforts to shore up the roofs have revived the area. The Catholic Church has also spent much time and money resurrecting the exteriors and interiors of the many churches housed within the old walls. **Tvrđa** was originally

Jasenovac Camp

Jasenovac is a name that stains the 20th-century history of Croatia and that continues to simmer below the surface today. The World War II concentration camp that was built in the woods southwest of Zagreb on the way to Slavonia had thousands of Serbs, Jews and other 'undesirables' put to death amid savage conditions. Much debate in the 1970s and 1980s focused on how many hundreds of thousands were killed here, but these squabbles are just a background to the brute fact of the camp's existence. Jasenovac was occupied by Serbian forces during the Homeland War and many of the surviving objects were removed. A Memorial Museum (Mar–Nov Tue–Fri 9am–5pm, Sat–Sun 10am–4pm, Dec–Feb Mon–Fri 9am–4pm; free) tells some of the horrifying stories of the victims.

built by the Habsburgs as a bulwark against the Ottoman Empire and its rich history is now starting to be unearthed.

Vukovar  is a name that conjures up a whole range of emotions in any Croat. It had been a pleasant Baroque town on the Danube inhabited by a mix of Croats, Serbs, Bosnians, Germans and Slovaks among others. Tragically for Vukovar it lay on the eastern edge of the new Republic of Croatia,

Church in Tvrđa, Osijek's old quarter

and in 1991 the political leaders in Belgrade conspired with local Serbs to 'ethnically cleanse' the town. Its devastation was one of the lowest points of the Homeland War.

Visiting Vukovar today gives a real sense of what happened to Croatia during the war – something that is not easy to appreciate in the glossy coastal resorts. The remaining residents soon dispel any doubts about whether it is distasteful to visit the town. They are only too happy to see outsiders who take an interest in the suffering that they felt was ignored by the rest of Europe. Tourism is crucial to the recovery of Vukovar and, on a larger scale, to Slavonia.

ISTRIA

Istria ❻, the triangular-shaped peninsula that extends into the Adriatic in the extreme north of the Croatian seaboard, is one of the country's most popular tourist destinations. Since the 1960s, visitors have been pouring into the purpose-built resorts in and around Rovinj, Vrsar, Umag, Novigrad and, the busiest of them all, Poreč. The Homeland War did

Vukovar still bears scars from the Homeland War

not directly affect Istria, and tourism has been back on track for some time with refurbished hotels and new developments. These include the *Agroturizam* programme, which has transformed old farmhouses into restaurants and small hotels.

Istria's principal city is Pula, whose fine amphitheatre is a reminder of the time when the Romans held sway over the peninsula. Their empire left numerous traces in Croatia, and the central cores of both Pula and Poreč are still built on the original Roman plan. The Venetians, too, left their mark on Istria, most notably in the coastal town of Rovinj and in the interior, where Venetian fortifications are the legacy of the days when pirates and Ottomans threatened the trade routes and the Istrian peninsula.

Pula

Croatia's Roman heritage is most impressive in **Pula**. The city's dramatic legacy from its days as Polensium is the **Roman Amphitheatre** (July–Aug 8am–12am, June–Sept 8am–9pm variable, Oct–March 8am–5pm; charge), standing proud near the waterfront. Originally the amphitheatre would have attracted 23,000 spectators to its bloody entertainment; today it is still pulling in the punters for rock and classical concerts and its annual film festival. A small museum is housed in the vaults, but the main attraction is just walking around with the ghosts of the Romans in this 2,000-year-old arena.

Finds from Polensium are displayed in the Archaeological Museum just south of the amphitheatre. Its Sculpture Garden forms a delightful venue for classical concerts in summer.

Other interesting remnants of Roman rule include the **Triumphal Arch of Sergius**, the **Temple of Augustus** and the remains of the **Roman Forum**. The tourist office offers maps detailing the most worthwhile sights of Polensium, traces of which can be found in such inauspicious places as the bus station, where the Roman walls can be seen.

Pula's **Cathedral of St Mary** is a testament to the eventual victory of Christianity over paganism here. Parts of it date from the 4th century, and some of it was built from stone lifted from the Roman amphitheatre after the demise of Polensium. The cathedral has undergone numerous renovations over the years, many of which can be easily traced, such as the 4th-century rear wall, the 13th-century sacristy and the 17th-century bell tower.

James Joyce

James Joyce aficionados may want to follow the trail left in Pula by the great Irish writer before he flitted north to Trieste and set about finishing *A Portrait of the Artist as a Young Man* and embarking on his epic *Ulysses*. The tourist office is keen to push the minimal Joyce connection, and the local branch of the Berlitz language school where he found work in 1904 is now open as the Uliks (Ulysses) Café. Outside the café is a bronze sculpture of Joyce sitting at his favourite chair, with his trademark hat and walking stick. The sculpture was designed by local artist Mate Čvrljak and it has become almost obligatory to have your photo taken with the author.

Not that Joyce was all that enamoured with Istria. In a letter from Pula dated 1904, he described Istria as 'a long boring place wedged into the Adriatic, peopled by ignorant Slavs who wear red caps and colossal breeches'.

Vodnjan

The road north to the resorts passes through **Vodnjan**, 10km (6 miles) from Pula. This fairly nondescript inland town is known for its 'mummies' in St Blaise's Church. Some devout Croats believe that the mummies possess magical powers, but many of today's visitors just come for the ghoulish appeal of viewing the desiccated corpses of St Nikolosa Bursa, St Giovanni Olini and St Leon Bembo. Vodnjan itself is worth a wander, and there are a couple of small restaurants if you want to stay for lunch or dinner.

Rovinj

About 50km (30 miles) north along the E751 from Pula is **Rovinj**, the most attractive town on the Istrian littoral. The approach to Rovinj is spectacular, with views of the old town clustered on a hilly peninsula in a collage of orange roof tiles and cobbled streets. In summer the streets can be busy, but the big hotel developments and campsites are outside the old town so much of the historical core remains unspoilt.

Dominating Rovinj from its highest spot is the church of **St Euphemia**. This 18th-century Baroque creation features Istria's tallest bell tower, which has been used for centuries by local fishermen for weather forecasts and as a landmark for seeking their way home. Legend has it that the body of St Euphemia arrived shrouded in mystery in her weighty sarcophagus on the Rovinj shoreline. No one could budge the bulky stone tomb

The Roman Amphitheatre in Pula

Rovinj

until a local boy and his two cows conspired with divine intervention to spirit her to her last resting place. The sarcophagus is now in the church.

The **Heritage Museum** (Zavičajni muzej; www.muzej-rovinj.com; high season Tue–Fri 9am–3pm and 7–10pm, Sat–Sun 9am–2pm and 7–10pm, low season Tue–Sat 10am–1pm; charge) makes a good attempt at delving into the town's history. As well as playing host to temporary exhibitions, it has a permanent collection of Istrian folk costumes and finds from local archaeological digs, as well as paintings from the 15th and 16th centuries. The highlight is Pietro Mera's *Christ Crowned with Thorns*.

For children, a good distraction outside the old town is **Rovinj Aquarium** (*Akvarij*; high season 9am–9pm, low season 10am–5pm; charge). The aquarium was opened in 1891, and although it is not exactly state of the art, it is home to a colourful collection of Istrian marine life.

Rovinj rooftops viewed from the church of St Euphemia

One of Rovinj's most appealing streets is **Grisia**, a narrow lane that sneaks north from sea level up to the church of St Euphemia. Grisia is charming enough in itself, with fine views of the church unfolding as you ascend, but it is also home to Rovinj's thriving artistic community. The enlightened local authorities have encouraged painters and craftsmen to live and work along Grisia, and more than a dozen small shops now have the artists' eclectic work on sale. Much of it is blatantly geared towards the tourist trade, but usually there are some interesting pieces to be found if you look carefully.

One of the great pleasures in Rovinj is doing nothing other than dipping in and out of the Adriatic Sea. As with many Istrian towns, there are no real beaches, only a ramble of rocks around the old town peninsula, as well as concrete platforms and steps for less agile bathers. Lining the waterfront on the southern side of the town are cafés and restaurants.

Poreč

About 30km (20 miles) north of Rovinj is **Poreč**, the epicentre of Istria's tourist industry, with attractive Venetian-style architecture. Despite throngs of holidaymakers, the old town retains its character because many of the area's hotels and campsites are located in the purpose-built resort of Zelena Laguna. In high season, Poreč's waterfront is lined with bobbing tour boats; the restaurants offer tourist menus and there are myriad watersports on offer.

Tourism apart, Poreč's greatest attraction is the Unesco World Heritage listed **Basilica of Euphrasius** (daily 7am–8pm; charge for bell tower), one of the most remarkable examples of Byzantine art in the world. The scattering of buildings inside the main complex occupy the site of a 4th-century church, whose mosaics can be seen in the apse just inside the main door of today's basilica. The ebullient gold and mother-of-pearl studded scenes of the Virgin and Child, the Annunciation and Visitation are captivating.

The Romans made Poreč what it is today with their sturdy town plan, and its main thoroughfares are still evident, though these days they are lined with shops, cafés and restaurants. Follow Decumanus down from Zagrebačka to trace the heart of the Roman town, a walk culminating at the Forum. Look out for the **Romanesque House**, built many centuries after the Romans left Istria and now housing an art gallery.

Istrian Wines

Ancient Greek settlers first brought wine production to Dalmatia, while in Istria, wine has been popular since Roman times. Under the Communists, the focus was placed on quantity over quality, and then during the Croatian War of Independence in the early 1990s, many vineyards were destroyed. Since the 1990s, burgeoning boutique wineries and growing brands have brought Croatian wine back to the international market. Large-scale producers and small family-run vineyards have invested in modern machinery and techniques, improving the standards of what were already fine wines.

Look out for Muscatel and Malvazija whites and the Teran red. These wines are available in shops all over Istria, though they are expensive when bottled – which is why many locals travel out to vineyards themselves to buy in bulk. The Istria County Tourist Association has produced the Guide to the Wine Roads of Istria with a map and details of the vineyards where you can sample and buy wine. It is available from tourist offices in Istria.

Other Coastal Resorts

Development is continuing along the coast. Between Rovinj and Poreč is **Vrsar**, a quieter resort than Poreč.

To the north of Poreč towards the Slovenian border are the resorts of **Umag** and **Novigrad**. Novigrad is the more attractive of the two – a sort of mini-Rovinj complete with a bell tower overlooking a town that curls around a peninsula. Though there are some unattractive hotel developments dating from the communist era, there is a marina and some good fish restaurants. Umag is appealing in a different way, and has its moment in the spotlight every July when the Croatian Tennis Open brings in big international names, as well as local stars.

On Istria's quieter east coast, hillside **Labin** is the largest and most interesting settlement. Its neighbour, **Rabac**, offers excellent beaches and lively nightlife.

The exquisite mosaics in the Basilica of Euphrasius in Poreč

Boat Trips from the Coastal Resorts

Between May and October there are regular boat excursions from all the Istrian resorts. The trips often include lunch and can be booked at hotels or at the boats themselves on the previous evening, or even, subject to availability, on the day. One of the most popular excursions is to the **Brijuni Islands**, www. brijuni.hr, a string of verdant islands that were given national park status in 1983.

Novigrad waterfront houses

Public access is allowed on only two of them, Veli Brijun and Mali Brijun; even then visitors either have to be staying at one of the hotels on Veli Brijun or be on one of the organised tours.

The islands were once a retreat for Tito, who spent much of his time entertaining world dignitaries here. These guests are said to have brought many of the animals at Brijuni Zoo as gifts for the communist leader.

Limski Zaljev (Lim Fjord) is one of the most dramatic day trips. The steep walls of the fjord are covered with lush vegetation, and were once a hideaway for pirates and the setting for Richard Widmark's 1963 Viking film, *The Long Ships*. Its waterside restaurants are an excellent place for lunch, particularly the Viking, which was named after the film and displays some of its memorabilia. Visitors with their own transport can also take the old road from Rovinj to Poreč and stop off to savour some of the best seafood in Croatia.

Brijuni Islands ferry

Istrian Interior

While the coast attracts the holidaymakers, the hinterland remains mostly unexplored. The rolling green landscape of scenic hill towns and winding roads is blessed with many fine wines, truffles to match the best Italy and France have to offer, and rustic places to savour the food and drink of the region. It is being dubbed the 'New Tuscany' and is where Agroturizam is opening up traditional farmhouses as restaurants and guesthouses (see page 112).

A 35km (22-mile) drive east of Poreč is Istria's rather unlikely regional capital, **Pazin**, which is a good base for exploring the interior, although it is by no means as attractive as many of the smaller hill towns. The main sights in the town are the castle, incorporating the Ethnographic Museum of Istria and the town museum (www.emi.hr; high season daily 10am–6pm; low season times vary and closed Sunday and Monday; charge), and the plunging limestone gorge that descends more than 100m (328ft) below the town centre. This vertiginous drop was said to have been the inspiration for Jules Verne when he propelled the eponymous protagonist of his novel *Mathias Sandorf* over the abyss. Some say the spectacular chasm may also have prompted Dante to write his *Inferno*.

The archetypal Istrian hill town is **Motovun**, situated 20km (12 miles) northeast of Poreč, and now well known for its annual film festival. Motovun has it all: the vineyards on the approach through the valley of the Mirna River and the winding road up the green slopes to an orange-roofed old town that harbours Roman and Venetian remnants. There are cosy cafés and small restaurants where the local cuisine can be sampled. The best way to get acquainted with Motovun is to take to its Venetian walls and wander around the old stone defences, surveying the tiled rooftops on one side and the rolling countryside on the other. Look out for the small village of Livade just below Motovun, where the truffle company Zigante Tartufi is based.

Buzet is also renowned for its high-quality truffles. Every September there is a truffle festival, and in season the men and their dogs can be seen heading out into the forests hunting for the pungent delicacy. Restaurants all over Istria serve truffles with pasta as well as steak with black truffle sauce. Those who are self-catering may like to buy truffle products at the Zigante Tartufi outlets in Pula, Buzet, Livade and Buje.

Grožnjan, to the west of Motovun, is a shining example of what can be done with a crumbling old town by forward-thinking

Pazin is perched on a limestone cliff

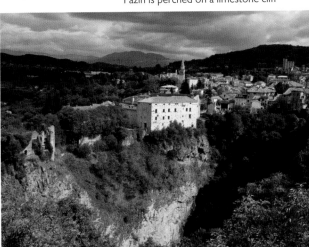

Motovun

local authorities. Grožnjan was slowly dying until artists and craftsmen were tempted into its narrow cobbled streets by the promise of free or low rents and refurbished houses. Today, the art scene flourishes with dozens of workshops. An international summer college for young musicians is based in Grožnjan, and this hilly outcrop is often bathed in the sounds of classical music. The town is pedestrianised, making it ideal for an unhurried morning or afternoon browsing through the workshops.

About 40km (25 miles) east of Grožnjan is **Hum**, billed as the smallest town in the world – it has just one circular street and square accommodating the houses, post office, church and other essentials that qualify it as a town. Now that it has cottoned on to its place in the world, this charming settlement is making the most of it.

KVARNER GULF

The Kvarner Gulf is the wide island-studded basin that separates the Istrian peninsula in the north from the Dalmatian regions in the south. In some ways it offers the best of both areas, with well-developed resort facilities and rustic towns to explore. Transport links are good, too: the motorway stretches from Zagreb to Rijeka (toll fee) and much of

Dalmatia, and there are ferry services to Dalmatia and train links from Zagreb to Rijeka.

The most interesting areas of the Kvarner Gulf are the coastal towns and the islands, whereas much of the hinterland is unforgiving and undeveloped. The harsh face of the interior is omnipresent with the voluminous wall of the Velebit range hanging over the gulf and bringing in summer thunderstorms and the bitter *bura* wind. The Velebit mountains also give walkers and mountaineers spectacular views over the Kvarner Gulf.

Rijeka

Situated on the Kvarner Gulf's northern shore, **Rijeka** is the principal city in the region and an important transport hub, with a major ferry terminal and an airport on the nearby island of Krk. The town experienced a golden age as a thriving Adriatic port under the Habsburg empire. From the 19th century, trains linked it to Vienna and Budapest. Today this industrial metropolis is making a concerted effort to tempt tourists to stay for a day or two rather than breeze through in search of the next ferry or bus. Its harbour terminal includes a restaurant and nightclub, and the annual Rijeka Carnival, which takes place in January and February each year, attracts a huge crowd.

View over the Kvarner Gulf

Rijeka's main thoroughfare is the elegant Korzo, home to many of its best shops, cafés and most impressive buildings. To get a feel for the city, idle for a while at a café and survey the scene.

Then venture into **Stari Grad** (old town) through the medieval City Tower and you'll come upon another world, far removed from the 19th-century order outside. This scruffy historic quarter has a Roman arch, as well as the church of **St Vitus**, dedicated to the city's patron saint. Parts of the church date from the 17th century and were modelled on Santa Maria della Salute Basilica in Venice.

For a sweeping view of the city, take a bus up the steep hill to the 13th-century castle at **Trsat**, or tackle the 561 steps. This may not be one of Europe's most attractive castles, but the views are good and in summer there are classical concerts in the grounds and a pleasant open-air café. Nearby, the church of **Our Lady of Trsat** is a place of pilgrimage, particularly for women whose messages of thanks and pleas for help line the interior. Legend has it that this church was where the House of Mary and Joseph came to rest in the 13th century after fleeing Nazareth en route to Italy. It is said to have remained on the site where the church is today for three years before continuing its journey across the Adriatic.

The Opatija Riviera

The eastern extremity of the Istrian peninsula, a short drive west of Rijeka, was a favourite playground for the 19th-century Viennese, who came here to escape the winter cold and seek cures for their various ailments. With a famously mild climate afforded by its unparalleled setting between the Adriatic and the Učka Mountains, it is easy to see its attraction.

Opatija itself is one of the few year-round coastal resorts in Croatia, with a growing choice of luxury hotels and good restaurants. The town has retained many of its grand 19th-century hotel buildings, as well as the Lungomare, a waterfront promenade that is packed with people in summer and is still a pleasant place for strolls even in winter. The graceful waterfront gardens and elegant buildings still speak of the affluent days when Opatija became one of Europe's top tourist destinations, not least following the completion of the rail line from Vienna to Trieste in 1873.

The Lungomare connects Opatija with **Volosko** to the north and **Lovran** to the south. Sleepy Volosko makes for an enjoyable morning stroll, particularly if you reward your efforts with lunch in one of its seafood restaurants. Lovran is a mini-Opatija with some hotels and buildings that hark back to the riviera's golden age. There are good cafés and restaurants and opportunities for bathing. Lovran is also a good base if you are planning to walk in the **Učka mountains**;

Adriatic view in Opatija

View over Baška on the island of Krk

information is available from the local tourist office.

Paklenica National Park

The scenery southeast of Rijeka is spectacular, with the Velebit mountain range towering above the barren coast, but there are few attractions other than the small town of **Senj**. In the 16th century, Senj became infamous as the base from which the Uskok warriors would set forth to attack shipping on the Adriatic.

Further south, the **Paklenica National Park** ❼ (www. paklenica.hr; charge) is a paradise for walkers, mountaineers and rock climbers. From the town of Starigrad a series of trails caters for all levels of agility and ability. The park is well organised and information and maps are obtainable from the national park office in Starigrad, which is where hotels are based. If you are planning a long hike, basic mountain hut-style accommodation is available, but hotels (and hunting) are banned from the park. There are two main gorges: Mala Paklenica and Velika Paklenica, literally 'small' and 'big' Paklenica. The latter is the more user-friendly, with a well-marked main trail that snakes up in a 2-hour walk from the car park. Climbers can start off with the sheer rock face that greets visitors at the entrance to the park.

Kvarner Gulf Islands

Krk ❽ is a popular island, particularly among Austrians, Hungarians and Germans, for whom it is an easy drive south and across the bridge (toll fee). **Krk Town** retains a semblance of its historic ambience with a solid old core and a few worthwhile churches. The nearby resort of **Baška** is the most appealing on the island, with 2km (1.2 mile) of Blue Flag beach and the brooding Velebit mountains visible on the mainland. As well as having modern hotels and campsites, Baška has a small old quarter with good seafood restaurants and pension-style accommodation. It is essential to book ahead in high season.

Baška is famous for the 12th-century Baška Tablet (now in the Academy of Arts and Science in Zagreb), the oldest existing example of Glagolitic script, the precursor of Cyrillic and used in Croatia until well into the Middle Ages.

Wine-lovers should head to the northeastern coastal town of Vrbnik. Set among high cliffs, this attractive town is home to some of Croatia's best white wines, namely vrbinčka žlahtina. Try it in one of the town's many wine cellars and restaurants.

A small car ferry departs daily in summer from Baška across the channel to the less-developed island of **Rab**, home to beautiful **Rab Town**. It is also possible to take a ferry from Jablanac in Northern Dalmatia across to Rab, which is worth considering if you are planning a journey along the coastline.

Hiking Opportunities

In addition to visiting Paklenica National Park, keen hikers may like to explore the rugged Mt Učka massif, accessible from towns along the coast between Poklon Pass in the north to Plomin Bay in the south. Facilities are not extensive, but there are a few mountain lodges and stone cottages for hikers, a restaurant at Poklon and a viewpoint tower on the peak of Vojak. For Vojak, the highest peak (1,394 metres/4,596ft), climb through Lovran's old town and follow the steps that lead up the hillside to the village of Liganj and on to the hamlets of Didici and Ivulici. The ascent can be managed in around four hours, but take provisions.

Rab's lovely old town

The island has a number of modest resorts and villages, but Rab Town is its undoubted star, with a well-preserved old quarter punctuated by church spires and cobbled streets. Swimming in the shadow of the pine trees beneath the old walls is a memorable experience. There are also regular taxi-boats serving beaches located in isolated bays around the island.

Rab Town's nightlife is amongst the liveliest on the Kvarner Gulf, making it popular with younger travellers. But it is also popular with families and the island has an unmistakable buzz in high season.

Although you can see **Pag** from Rab, and there is a catamaran service to Novalja on Pag, getting there can often be frustrating. For those staying in Rab Town, the island is best reached on an organised boat trip. Pag is famous for its lamb, sheep's milk cheese *(paški sir)*, found on menus throughout Croatia, and also for intricate hand-made lace. **Novalja** has a reputation for being one of Croatia's party towns, with a cluster of clubs around the beach. **Pag Town** is the best base for exploring the island.

Of the two main islands on the western side of the Kvarner Gulf – Cres and Lošinj – Cres is the most northerly, with ferry connections from Istria, Rijeka and Krk. **Cres Town** makes a good base for travelling the length of the island. Colourful houses encircle its busy harbour from where fishermen supply the local restaurants.

Lošinj lies across a narrow channel to the south of Cres. The two main towns are Mali and Veli Lošinj. **Mali Lošinj** is more developed and attracts those in search of louder bars and a choice of day trips. In contrast, **Veli Lošinj** has a more rustic appeal, but enough facilities to ensure an enjoyable stay. There are a number of islets dotted around Lošinj that can be explored by day, and by night Italian influenced seafood awaits at the waterfront restaurants of both towns.

DALMATIA

Dalmatia ❾ is the long sinewy arm of Croatia that sweeps southeast from the Kvarner Gulf towards the border with Montenegro, hugging the Bosnian border for much of its length. Its coastline is punctuated by historic cities and towns and littered with myriad offshore islands, each with its own

Dolphins of Lošinj

The dolphins of Lošinj attracted international attention with the launch of the award-winning Adriatic Dolphin Project in 1987. Covering the islands of Cres and Lošinj, the project aims to discover more about the dolphins' way of life, as well as to help in their protection. The crystal waters and rugged coastline are a haven for these delightful mammals, something that yachtsmen can confirm, with many passing boats enjoying a very special escort.

Swimming with dolphins is prohibited, but those wanting to get involved can volunteer to take part in the project. When the weather is suitable the time is spent out at sea recording, dating and tracking the creatures, and direct contact with them is common. In poor weather there are lectures and the chance to delve into the project's archives. For details see www.blue-world.org, where you can also 'adopt a dolphin'.

St Donat's Church

allure. The Homeland War hit parts of Dalmatia badly, and while the images of Dubrovnik being shelled made TV news bulletins around the world (see page 23), it was the northern cities of Zadar and Šibenik that fared worst.

Today much of the war damage has been repaired and you can spend a week or two in Dalmatia without noticing anything unusual. Compared to Istria, much of Dalmatia's tourist industry is pleasantly low key – with the major exception of Dubrovnik and islands such as Hvar, which are growing rapidly in popularity. There is plenty to see in a region where the only constants are outstanding scenery, rich layers of history and the omnipresent waters of the Adriatic.

Northern Dalmatia

During the Homeland War, **Zadar** ⑩ was cut off from the rest of the country as Serb forces pummelled the historic centre. Today the city is firmly back on its feet, with museums of interest, a revamped waterfront, hotels and lively nightlife.

Zadar's old town is spectacularly situated on a peninsula, its sturdy walls and lofty gates protecting it from attack. **Široka Ulica**, the arrow-straight Roman road that dissects the old town, passes many of the key sights as it makes its way west to the Adriatic. The post-World War II buildings that replaced those destroyed by Allied bombs are all too evident, but amid them is the Baroque church of **St Simeon**. Its treasure is the Romanesque sarcophagus by the Milanese goldsmith Francesco di Antonio da Sesto, embellished with reliefs depicting the life of the saint and the rescue of his relics from the Venetians by Louis I.

Further west is **Narodni Trg**, the square that took over from the Roman Forum as the hub of city life during the Middle Ages. Fronting the square is a Venetian-era **Town Loggia** (loža; Mon–Sat 8am–8pm, Sun 9am–1pm; free), housing an art gallery and temporary exhibitions. Also on the square is the 16th-century Guard House with its lofty clock tower, as well as a couple of pavement cafés. From Narodni Trg you can head north through the old Sea Gate and across a footbridge to the newer part of the city.

A 10-minute walk west along Široka Ulica from Narodni Trg brings you to the site of the Roman Forum. Here, among the stony remains of what was once Zadar's focal point, stands the city's symbol, **St Donat's Church** (times vary; charge). The cylindrical church was built in the 9th century using, in part, stones culled from the Roman Forum, which can be recognised by their Latin inscriptions. The compact two-storey interior, with its tightly packed stone walls, is unlike that of any other religious building in Croatia. Today it no longer functions as a place of worship, but in summer its fine acoustics can be appreciated when it is used as a venue for classical and folk music concerts.

Facing St Donat's Church across the Forum is the worthwhile **Archaeological Museum** (Arheološki muzej; daily 9am–9pm but varies in summer, in winter Mon–Fri 9am–2pm and Sat 9am–1pm but also varies; charge). On display are finds from excavations all over northern Dalmatia, with the Roman era in Zadar well represented.

Zadar Cathedral, on the northwestern side of the Forum, dates from the 12th century, although much on view today was painstakingly reconstructed after Allied bombing during World War II. The slightly incongruous-looking bell tower was a 19th-century addition to the Romanesque cathedral.

The **Zadar Museum of Antique Glass** (Muzej antičkog stakla; summer daily 9am–9pm, winter 9am–4pm; charge), in the refurbished 19th century Cosmacendi Palace, contains one of the best antique glassware collections outside Italy. Zadar's art installations on the Riva promenade have also attracted international acclaim. The *Sea Organ* consists of a series of stone steps leading into the sea, with underwater pipes creating the sound effects. The *Greeting to the Sun* creates an intricate light show on the surface of the promenade at sunset.

Zadar's beaches are north and south of the old town, with many rocky stretches among some gravel and sand. Borik and Diklo are north of the town, and Kolovare to the south is one of the most popular, combining sand and gravel. You'll find plenty of facilities for children including play areas.

About an hour's drive south of Zadar along the motorway or E65 is the city of **Šibenik**. Until the 1990s it was a major industrial centre, but the war put paid to the traditional enterprises and the city became one of the poorest in the country. Unusually for the Croatian coastline, there are no traces of Roman civilisation here as the city was established by the Croatian kings a millennium ago. Hence the jumbled streets of the old town and the low-rise muddle of houses, which are in contrast to the elegant order of Roman Poreč or Zadar. But the shape of its coastline made it a natural home for Croatia's first marina for super-yachts, D-Marin Mandalina, so some aspects of the city's economy are perking up.

The city's main attraction, dominating the city and skyline, is **Šibenik Cathedral** (times vary; free), a Unesco World Heritage Site. Much of the cathedral was the work of

Zadar-born Juraj Dalmatinac (c.1400–73), though it took over a century to build and has many different influences incorporated into its grand design, from late gothic to Renaissance. Also in the city centre are the restored medieval **garden of St Lawrence's Monastery** (times vary; free) and **Bunari – Secrets of Šibenik** (times vary; charge for exhibition), where buskers play, and an interactive exhibition tells the story of the city and its four wells, which helped the city through long periods of drought and siege.

Just outside Šibenik, in the village of Dubrava, is Croatia's only **Falconry Centre** (www.sokolarskicentar.com), where you can learn about the ancient art and the conservation of birds of prey. Half an hour's drive from Šibenik in the village of Pakovo Selo is **Etnoland** (www.dalmati.com), a well-designed discovery park revealing the secrets of Dalmatian life before the age of electricity.

Šibenik Cathedral

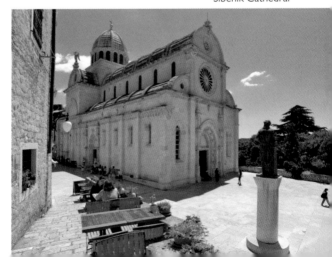

Around Zadar and Šibenik, the main resort areas of **Borik**, **Biograd**, **Solaris** and **Vodice** all have extensive resort facilities, and a range of hotels, restaurants and nightlife.

An hour's drive south along the motorway or E65 past the pretty resort of Primošten is **Trogir**, which also features on Unesco's World Heritage list, and justifiably so. Trogir's old quarter is a beautifully preserved medieval oasis set on its own islet. In high season, holidaymakers throng the old streets of 14th- and 15th-century buildings, relaxing in the seafood restaurants and watching the luxury yachts come and go from the cafés along the Riva promenade.

Trogir's most impressive attraction is its **cathedral** (times vary; charge for bell tower). The remarkable 13th-century west portal is the work of Croatian sculptor Master Radovan and depicts scenes from the life of Christ as well as images of local Dalmatian life. Inside is the superb Renaissance Chapel of St John, created by Nikola Firentinac, with its 160 sculpted heads of angels, cherubs and saints.

In and around the cathedral square you can also admire the **Čipiko Palace**, **town hall**, **loggia** and **clock tower** and, nearby, the crumbling remains of **Kamerlengo Castle** (times vary; charge), now used as an open-air cinema and events stage. You can walk up the stairs and admire the views.

Connected to Trogir by bridge is the small island of Čiovo, lined with pebbly beaches around the villages of Arbanije, Slatine. Scuba-divers are catered for along the beaches at Okrug Donji and Okrug Gornji. To visit one of the few sandy beaches in the region, take a boat ride from Trogir to the tiny island of Drvnek Mali.

An easy day trip inland from Zadar, Šibenik or Trogir is **Krka National Park ⓫** (www.npkrka.hr; charge includes boat ride from Skradin to Skradinski Buk). This natural wonderland of gorges and waterfalls on the River Krka may be lesser known than the Plitvice Lakes further north, but it is every bit as appealing and not usually as busy. From the village of **Skradin**, 16km (10 miles) from Šibenik, regular boats leave for the impressive **Skradinski Buk** and its 17 separate falls. From Skradinski Buk additional cruises venture deeper into the park (additional fee). **Visovac**, with its Franciscan monastery set in the midst of Visovačko Lake, is alone worth the trip. Housed in the monastery's library is an ornately illustrated copy of *Aesop's Fables*, thought to be one of only three of its kind in the world. Most cruises continue on to **Roški Slap**, another waterfall.

Another highlight of the region is the **Kornati Islands National Park** (www.kornati.hr). George Bernard Shaw eulogised dreamily at the beauty of the 147 barren, inhospitable and waterless strips of rugged rock that make up the archipelago.

Skradinski Buk falls, Krka National Park

Kornat, which stretches some 25km (15 miles) in length and 2.5km (1.55 miles) in width, is the largest; others are little more than rugged rocks, their stark terrain shining like beacons against the blue of the Adriatic. The national park is accessible on day trips from many northern Dalmatian towns and resorts, particularly Murter. But undoubtedly the best way to savour the archipelago is to spend a week sailing in their challenging waters, stopping off at rustic restaurants and secluded bays.

There are also some lovely undiscovered islands an easy ferry or boat trip from Šibenik. **Prvić** and **Krapanj** each have boutique hotels and, together with **Zlarin** and the smaller surrounding islands, are popular for swimming holidays as the islands are close to each other and low lying.

The Zadar archipelago has some 300 islands, the largest of which is Dugi otok. Its rocky coastline hides secluded coves and picturesque fishing ports, with its southeastern tip taken over by the Telašćica nature park and its numerous islets and exquisite bays.

Diocletian's Palace
cathedral bell tower

Southern Dalmatia: Split

Dalmatia's largest city, **Split ⑫**, was founded by the Roman emperor Diocletian in AD295. His retirement palace, the remarkably intact complex of **Diocletian's Palace Ⓐ** – a Unesco World Heritage Site – still forms the core of the city. Many of the original palace buildings have long since gone, although remnants of the basement rooms can be

Split's old town

seen. Today, cafés, bars, shops, hotels and apartments jostle for space within the palace's protective outer walls, which enclose the old town.

In the palace complex is the octagonal **Cathedral of St Domnius** (Sv Duje Katedrala; Mon–Sat 7am–noon, 4–7pm), which was originally built as Diocletian's mausoleum but later converted into a church. A black granite Egyptian sphinx can be seen to the right of the doorway. The cathedral's wooden doors were carved in 1214 by Andrija Buvina, a local sculptor, and depict scenes from the life of Christ. You can climb the Romanesque bell tower (charge) for bird's-eye views.

The cathedral overlooks the **Peristyle**, a colonnaded sunken square housing a café and restaurant that offers an atmospheric setting for refreshment.

North of Diocletian's Palace, through the **Golden Gate** (Zlatna Vrata), which originally led to the Roman town of Salona (see page 68), is the monumental sculpture of the

10th-century bishop Grgur of Nin (Gregory of Nin) by Ivan Meštrović (1929). Tradition claims that if you touch the statue's toe, a wish will be granted – the said toe is now a golden colour, burnished over the years by the hands of passers-by. Opposite the statue is the purpose-built, high-tech **Split Gallery of Modern Art** Ⓑ (www.galum.hr; May–Sept Mon 11am–4pm, Tue–Fri 11am–7pm, Sat 11am–3pm; Oct–Apr Mon 9am–2pm, Tue–Fri 9am–5pm, Sat 11am–3pm; charge) housing an incredible selection of masterpieces.

For an insight into the life and work of the Split-born sculptor, the **Meštrović Gallery** (Galerija Meštrovića; 46 Šetalište Ivana Meštrovića; high season Tue–Sun 9am–7pm, low season Tue–Sat 9am–4pm, Sun 10am–3pm; charge), situated beneath the Marjan peninsula to the west of the town, features some of his most important work. It is housed in what was the sculptor's summer home.

Split is known for its vibrant nightlife, which centres on Diocletian's Palace until 10pm, after which, in summer, the bars and clubs that line the waterfront to the south become the focal point. Earlier in the evening, locals of all ages like to promenade along **Marmontova**, stopping off at one of the many open-air cafés that line the Riva.

A short walk away from the centre and the ferry terminal is the **Bačvice** complex, around Split's gently sloping sandy beach. Here, and in nearby **Zenta**, are a clutch of good restaurants and cafés looking out to sea.

About 5km (3 miles) inland from Split and accessible by local bus are the ruins of the once thriving Roman town of **Salona** (times vary; charge). As the attacks of the Slavs in the 7th century took their toll on Salona, the citizens fled to Diocletian's Palace, thus ensuring its survival and the life that today still bustles within its stone walls. Remains dot the landscape of Salona, such as the amphitheatre that in its heyday played host to a baying 18,000-strong crowd.

The waterfront at Makarska

A few miles north of Split are the sleepy villages of **Kaštela**, named after the fortifications that dominate each of the seven villages. Some of the stone houses have been snapped up and renovated by foreigners for their old-world charms and magnificent views across Kaštela bay.

South of Split

South of Split is **Omiš**, the centre of Dalmatia's pirate history and its folk music (klapa), where an annual folk festival is held each summer. The scenery here is stunning and dramatic. The Biokovo mountains appear to spring directly from the old town itself as they rise steeply around the Cetina river gorge, making the area popular with hikers, mountaineers and river rafters. Further along, tumbling down the hillside from the road towards the pine-fringed Adriatic beaches are the various resorts and towns of the **Makarska Riviera**. Offshore the Dalmatian islands of Brač and Hvar laze in the Adriatic sun. Such glorious scenery makes up for the occasional bland town, ugly development and the numerous campsites along this stretch of coast.

The most attractive of the smaller resorts is **Brela**, at the northern end of the Riviera. **Makarska** itself is a big, brash place with good shingle beaches nearby and a vibrant nightlife. Resorts to the south include **Tučepi**, **Podgora**, **Drvenik** and **Zaostrog**.

South of Makarska the Magistrala road takes a brief sojourn through Bosnia (note that passports may be checked here), before re-emerging into Croatia and dropping down towards the **Pelješac peninsula**. This unspoilt spit of land juts out into the Adriatic Sea and provides some of the best wines in Croatia, such as *Dingač* and *Postup*, as well as first-rate seafood. **Ston** is linked to Mali Ston by 14th-century fortifications, about half of which still remain, built to protect the saltpans from mainland marauders. It is well worth breaking the journey here or making a special trip from Dubrovnik to absorb the history and savour the oysters and mussels that are farmed in front of the restaurants.

Dubrovnik

Widely considered to be one of Europe's most outstanding cities, **Dubrovnik** ⓭ is an integrated walled city with immense visual appeal. Its historical and architectural significance has been recognised by Unesco, which has placed it on its list of World Heritage sites. During the Homeland War, the city was under siege for six months and the tourist industry was decimated. Now, however, it has the opposite problem of too many visitors, many of whom are on day trips from the resorts or on cruises. In summer, the old town is very congested, and those turning up without somewhere to stay will almost certainly be disappointed.

The city's history has been shaped by its perpetual struggle to retain its independence. Settlement in the area first took

Inside Dubrovnik's city walls

root in the 7th century when Dubrovnik was an island cut off from the mainland by a small channel. Its original name of Ragusa translates as 'rock', and the former moniker still appears on flags and museums in the city. Even today, its citizens are proud that Dubrovnik's sturdy fortifications have never been breached, though in truth the city owed its freedom more to the skill of its diplomats than to its military strength. For centuries it was a major trading centre, with ships flitting all over the Mediterranean and beyond; by the 15th century, its boundaries extended as far as Ston to the north and to Cavtat in the south.

In 1667, a massive earthquake ripped through the region. The damage to Dubrovnik was devastating, with the old core of the city, including its fine Renaissance buildings, practically levelled and more than 5,000 people killed. The rebuilding programme was fortunately carefully managed, resulting in the fine baroque centre that we see today. But the city never really regained its former strength as a trading power and at the beginning of the 19th century came under the influence of Napoleonic France. It declined into a sleepy backwater until the 20th century, when tourists first started taking an interest. Today, its tourist industry is as slick and good at making money as its merchants were in the 16th century.

To get a real feel for Dubrovnik, you need to take to the **medieval walls** (May–Sept 8am–7pm, Oct–Apr 9am–3pm; charge) that envelop the old town, opening up vignettes of local life and providing a bird's-eye view of all of the main attractions. The climb is quite steep in parts as the sturdy walls rise up the hillside from the **Pile Gate Ⓐ**, the main entrance to the city, before running along a ridge and descending past the **Ploče Gate**. The southern walls plunge towards the Adriatic and make for great photos at sunset.

Stradun Ⓑ, also known as Placa, is the polished artery that runs through the heart of Dubrovnik, with sights to the left and right and a sprinkling of pleasant pavement cafés. Prijeko, the narrow street running parallel to Stradun, becomes an almost continuous line of restaurants in season, their tables packed with diners.

At the western extremity of Stradun is the **Great Fountain of Onofrio**, the culmination of a system that has brought fresh water to the city since 1444. The circular domed well, with its 16 water-spouting stone heads, is named after its designer Onofrio della Cava, an Italian who worked in the Dubrovnik region. According to some, it is lucky to drink at the well, but it was originally intended merely for washing on entering the city. A more minor fountain, known as the **Small Fountain of Onofrio**, is near the church of St Blaise (see page 74).

To the east, Stradun leads to **Luža Square**, site of a cluster of historic buildings. The 16th-century **Sponza Palace Ⓒ** (times vary; free) served as a bank, customs house, mint and treasury, before its current role as home to the state archives. This remarkable collection records the history and administration of Ragusa from the 13th century until its fall at the beginning of the 19th century. A shop selling facsimiles of historical documents is found in the palace's courtyard, as is the Memorial Room to the Defenders of Dubrovnik, with portraits of those who died during the 1991–2 siege. The courtyard is an atmospheric venue for musical performances during the Dubrovnik Festival in August.

At the southern end of Luža Square stands **Orlando's Column** (also known as Roland's Column) dating from 1418. It commemorates a mysterious figure who is said to have helped fight off Saracen pirates in the 8th century and, in doing so, earned the city's eternal gratitude. Orlando continues to play his part in Dubrovnik life as his column is where the start of the Dubrovnik Festival is declared every year.

Opposite is the 18th-century church of **St Blaise** (Crkva Sv Vlaho; opening times vary; free), named after the patron saint of Dubrovnik. Above the high altar stands a silver figure of St Blaise holding a scale model of the city: look out for similar representations of the saint elsewhere in the city.

Cloister of the Franciscan monastery

A short walk from the church is the **Rector's Palace** ❷ (Knežev Dvor; daily 9am–6pm; charge). This palatial building is a fitting residence for a figure who, in theory at least, was the most powerful person in the city. However, the honour of being rector was modified slightly by the fact that his family was not allowed to live with him and he was forbidden from leaving the palace unless on official business.

Constructed in the mid-15th century, the palace was the seat of the Ragusan government as well as housing a lethal gunpowder store that ignited with devastating effect on a couple of occasions. The present building dates mainly from 1739 and is in Baroque style with a few gothic details. On the ground floor of the palace are prison cells and on the upper floor are the state apartments and the former courtroom and judicial chambers. The palace's atrium makes a lovely concert venue.

Nearby is the **cathedral** (times vary according to season and services; charge for treasury), which was almost totally destroyed by the earthquake of 1667. The interior comes alive with dramatic celebrations of Mass and classical concerts during the Dubrovnik Festival. Note the compelling *Assumption* by Titian on the main altar. The adjoining treasury displays a horde of gold reliquaries, including the Byzantine skull case of St Blaise. A local legend tells of how Richard the Lionheart was saved from a shipwreck while returning from the Crusades and by way of thanks funded the building of the first cathedral.

In a narrow side street between the Stradun and Prijeko, near Pile Gate, **War Photo Limited** (www.warphotoltd.com; June–Sept daily 9am–9pm, May and Oct Tue–Sun 10am–4pm; charge) is a slick gallery devoted to photojournalism from war zones around the world.

Most of Dubrovnik's other sites are in the very compact area inside the city walls, mostly off Stradun or Luža Square. They include the Franciscan and Dominican monasteries, the Maritime Museum, the Rupe Granary (housing the Ethnographic Museum), the Jesuit Church and the city's synagogue. Outside the town, the **Homeland War Museum** on the site of the Imperial Fort at the top of Srđ mountain is worth a visit even just for the view itself. The Dubrovnik Cable Car (www.dubrovnikcablecar.com) is an easy, if someway pricey, way to reach the summit.

The city is at its liveliest during the **Dubrovnik Festival** (www.dubrovnik-festival.hr), held mid-July to mid-August. This arts extravaganza features theatre, opera and musical performances, and many historical buildings are opened as venues.

Those with a few days in Dubrovnik may want to make a refreshing trip over to the beaches of the wooded island of **Lokrum**, just offshore. Boats run regularly to the island, where visitors are not allowed to stay overnight. **Cavtat**, on the mainland near the airport, is a popular and quieter holiday destination, with an attractive waterfront lined with cafés and restaurants. It makes a great base for diving and attracts a number of luxury yachts. The village juts out on the edge of a peninsula, where boats from Dubrovnik regularly arrive. Buses to Cavtat are a less scenic – and less expensive – option.

Dalmatian Islands

The city of Split is a good base for exploring the Dalmatian Islands. Most people head straight for the island beaches, but don't ignore the settlements and rustic restaurants inland where island life started, away from marauding pirates.

Just half an hour across the water is **Brač**, Croatia's third largest island, featuring Bol's **Zlatni Rat** (Golden Cape), the country's best-known shingle beach. This cuts scenically into the Adriatic, attracting countless sun-worshippers and windsurfers. **Bol** itself has a pleasant old town and is a centre for walks in the surrounding hills. A longer walk, or a short drive by car and a reasonably challenging hour's walk from the car park, takes you to the time capsule of **Hermitage Blaca**. Originally a cave shelter for two monks who arrived from the mainland in 1551, it became a flourishing monastery until the last monk, an acclaimed astronomer, died in 1963. Strikingly cut into the rocks, the buildings and other historic treasures have been preserved as a museum.

Brač has become something of a centre for extreme sports, even hosting its own festival every summer. Vanka Regule Festival (www.vanka regule.com) takes place in June or July and includes free climbing and free diving in addition to more traditional sports such as mountain biking.

Dubrovnik viewed
from above

The neighbouring island of **Hvar** ⑭ is a favourite with international celebrities and has become one of Croatia's most visited destinations. **Hvar Town** attracts most of the attention as well-heeled people throng its cafés, restaurants and growing number of expensive nightclubs. They pile into the Riva that leads around the busy little harbour to the 16th-century St Stephen's Cathedral that dominates the main square. As its popularity grows, so do its prices, which are markedly higher in Hvar Town than in other parts of the Adriatic. The unassuming town of Stari Grad, the latest addition to Unesco's World Heritage list for its old town and plain, is the place to enjoy the

Tito's HQ

Tito set up base in a cave on Vis during World War II. From here he conducted many military operations and also hosted Churchill's envoy.

island's slower pace and less showy cultural life. In this sunniest of Croatia's islands, lavender is one of its biggest industries, with most of the production coming from small family-owned plots.

Just off Brač's west coast lies the smaller and almost completely undiscovered island of **Šolta**, a mass of olive groves and vineyards with a handful of sleepy settlements. The most notable is west-facing Maslinica, with its beautiful sunsets and upmarket hotel and restaurant in the restored 18th century Baroque castle.

Vis is the furthest island from the Croatian mainland and is quite unlike any of the others. It was first populated by the Greeks in the 4th century BC. Many of Europe's major powers have fought over it down the centuries including Austria, Italy, Germany and Britain, the latter two during World War II. Tourism was restricted here until 1989, as the island was used as a Yugoslav naval base. As a result, its population density is low compared with other parts of Croatia. In spite of its small size, the island is renowned for its wine production, with wine tastings offered in family-run cellars.

Hvar's main square

Vis Town curves around a bay with its most appealing quarter, Kut, where wealthy Venetians built their homes during the 16th century. The Franciscan monastery features gravestones by the celebrated Croatian sculptor Ivan Rendić (1849–1932), as well as a mass grave for Austrian sailors killed in a sea battle off Vis in 1866.

Across the mountains from Vis Town is the fishing village of **Komiža**. As you approach, the church of St Nicholas, on a vine-covered bluff, offers a shady respite from the summer heat; its nearby cemetery contains the ornate tombs of notable local families. In Komiža itself there is a modest

Maritime Museum (times vary; charge) that testifies to the town's fruitful association with the Adriatic. From Komiža you can take a boat trip in summer to the islet of **Biševo**, where, at around noon, the Blue Grotto (Modra špilja) is illuminated by a brilliant blue light, similar to the celebrated Blue Cave off Capri.

Further along the coastline, the island of **Korčula** ⑮ perches on the western end of the western end of the Pelješac peninsula (see page 70). **Korčula Town** is one of the most attractive settlements on the coastline, jutting out from the mountains on its own peninsula. It can be visited on a lengthy day trip from Dubrovnik, but is also an excellent place to spend a few days. Surrounded by solid medieval walls, the old town is laid out on a tight grid system. The locals claim that the legendary explorer Marco Polo hails from the town, and you can visit the **Marco Polo House** (times vary; charge) where the explorer is said to have been born. **St Mark's Cathedral** combines Gothic and Renaissance styles and contains an *Annunciation* by Tintoretto, who spent time in Korčula as a student.

The island is dotted with several very good beaches, including the sandy beach about a 15-minute walk from Korčula Town at Luka Korčulanska. To the south are several beaches near Lumbarda and towards the west at the village of Blato.

Korčula is the birthplace of Croatia's traditional sword dance, the moreška, and performances are held in the small outdoor theatre in Korčula Town (Monday and Thursday in high season).

South towards Dubrovnik, the island of **Mljet** is often overlooked, but not by Croatians who are very aware of its green and lush beauty. The **Mljet National Park**, (www.np-mljet. hr) centres upon two beautiful lakes, Malo Jezero (small lake) and Veliko Jezero (big lake), which are excellent for swimming, with crystal clear water and the shade of evergreen forests on the water's edge. There is a cycling path around one of the lakes and it is possible to go on a boat trip out to **St Mary's Island** to visit its **monastery**, an atmospheric spot with a restaurant and café.

Nearer to Dubrovnik are the **Elaphite Islands**, a cluster of quiet settlements surrounded by evergreen vegetation and popular sandy beaches. **Koločep** is the nearest to Dubrovnik and the smallest of the three inhabited islands, with two tiny villages, peaceful olive groves to wander past and a compact beach. **Lopud** is more developed for tourists, with more sandy beaches on which to relax. **Šipan** is the largest, its grand palaces a reminder of when Dubrovnik nobles used the island as their summer retreat. All three islands get very busy in the summer with day-trippers from Dubrovnik, but time your visit right for a delicious lunch of fresh seafood.

Vis monastery

WHAT TO DO

There is no shortage of activities on offer in Croatia. If you're looking for something adventurous, the Adriatic coast is a paradise for scuba diving, sailing and other water-sports. Inland you can go rafting and canoeing on the rivers or hiking and climbing in the mountains. There are beaches to relax on, islands to discover and historic walled cities to explore. Festivals give insights into local arts and culture; shopping, entertainment and nightlife are all to be enjoyed.

SPORTS

Diving

Croatia is one of Europe's top scuba-diving destinations. There are dive centres all the way along the Croatian coastline from **Umag** and **Rovinj** in Istria to **Dubrovnik** and **Cavtat** in southern Dalmatia. The highlight for many is the island of **Vis**, which has several diveable shipwrecks just off its coast and the **Blue Grotto** at Biševo (see page 80).

Other favourite destinations for divers are the **Kornati Islands**, **Mezanj island** near Dugi Otok, **Rovinj** and, to the south, the shipwreck of the *Tottono*, which was lost off the Dalmatian coast near Dubrovnik during World War II.

Scuba diving is strictly regulated in Croatia and no one is allowed to dive without first obtaining a diving certificate, which costs 100kn. To dive independently, as opposed to with a registered diving centre, requires further permission, which costs 2,400kn. Both certificates are valid for one year.

For more information contact the Croatian Tourist Board (www.croatia.hr); the website includes a diving section.

Dubrovnik Summer Festival event at the Rector's Palace

Sailing

Croatia has become something of a paradise for yachting enthusiasts, with Bill Gates, Bernie Ecclestone and Luciano Benetton amongst those cruising around its Adriatic coastline in summer. Now there's a vast choice of boats, sailing schools and small cruise boats.

The **islands around Split** offer short distances and plenty of shelter to those learning the ropes, whilst the **Kornati islands** provide challenging navigation but beautiful scenery. Experienced sailors enjoy the winds around **Pelješac**, though everyone pays attention when the *bura* wind starts to blow.

There are 55 marinas along the coast from Umag in the north of Istria to Cavtat in the very south of the country. Adriatic Croatian International (aci; www.aci-club.hr) is the biggest operator with 21 marinas. Some of the larger marinas are almost resorts in themselves, while others, such as those at Trogir and Rab, bring you right into the heart of the town.

Would-be sailors have the choice of going 'bareboat' by just chartering a boat themselves, or taking a skipper. For bareboat you will need at least one member of your party to be a qualified skipper who can use a VHF radio. If you choose the skippered option, the cost goes up and you have to take one less person along in your party as the hired skipper will also sleep aboard. The toughest parts of sailing, such as navigation, will be taken out of your hands, though you and other members of your party will be required to help out with the ropes.

The website of the Croatian National Tourist Office – www.croatia.hr – has a comprehensive section on sailing.

Other Watersports

All the coastal resorts offer watersports, especially in Istria where larger hotels lay on everything from **waterskiing to**

Yachts at Korčula

parasailing. Or you can simply go **snorkelling** in the crystal clear Adriatic. Inland, the rivers Kupa and Cetina are suitable for both **rafting and canoeing**. Organised rafting trips set off regularly in season, subject to conditions.

Football

The most popular spectator sport in Croatia is undoubtedly football. Only seven years after declaring independence, Croatia achieved third place in the 1998 World Cup; a performance it has since struggled to match. The Croatian national team play most of their games at the Maksimir Stadium in Zagreb, but also sometimes travel to Split and Varaždin. **Dinamo Zagreb** also play at Maksimir, regularly doing well in their domestic league as well as playing in the Uefa Champions League. Their great rivals have always been **Hajduk Split** from the southern city and big games between the two can be turbulent affairs.

Rafting

Whitewater rafting is possible on several of Croatia's rivers. The Kupa River, near Karlovac, offers some of the best rafting in Central Croatia. Towards the Adriatic, in the Gorski Kotar, rafting can be arranged on the Dobra River. From the Dalmatian coast it is easy to get to the Cetina River, where rafting can be enjoyed in spring and summer.

Tennis

The other major spectator sport in Croatia is tennis, with key players such as Ivan Dodig and Marin Čilić drawing big crowds for their matches. One of the highlights of the tennis calendar is in July in Umag when the **Croatian Tennis Open** regularly attracts big names to an event that is becoming more popular every year.

There are also plenty of opportunities to play tennis. Every major coastal resort has tennis courts, and while many are affiliated to hotels, non-residents can also usually arrange a game for a fee. The excellent facilities at Umag host the Croatian Tennis Open, but when they are not in use for tournaments or training, they can be rented out, offering a rare chance for amateurs to play at an international tennis venue.

Walking, Hiking and Climbing

Croatia has a range of opportunities for walking and hiking. The most popular areas with mountaineers and those looking for a real challenge are the **Velebit range** and the sheer limestone walls of **Paklenica National Park**. The park has basic facilities and caters for all levels of climber, from beginner right through to serious mountaineers and daredevil free climbers. At the entrance to the main gorge a steep rock wall is used for practising, training and for showing first-timers the ropes.

Elsewhere, the **Risnjak National Park** at the northern end of Velebit is more suited to those intending to trek and hike. On the eastern edge of the Istrian peninsula, where it meets the Kvarner Gulf, **Mt Učka** is a good option for day trips from the resorts of Opatija and Labin. Southwest of Zagreb are the **Samobor Hills** where Tito first laced up his hiking boots.

SHOPPING

Croatia is slowly emerging as a good shopping destination, particularly in the bigger cities. **Zagreb and Dubrovnik** have a good range of designer stores and interesting shops, with **Split** and other cities catching up fast. Nearly everything is available here that you would find in any other major European city. The towns and villages have smaller outlets selling local produce and handicrafts, and in the coastal resorts the work of local artists is on sale.

Rock climbers at Paklenica National Park

Best Buys
Food and Drink

In Croatia, some locals refer to any food that is not organic as 'chicken feed', such is the prevalence of **organic produce** throughout the country. Under communism, much of the country's food was produced on a local small-scale or family basis; as a result the people take great pride in the quality and high standard of their produce.

Often the best places to buy the freshest fruit and vegetables are the **bountiful local markets**, still very much alive today despite the increasing number of shopping malls and supermarkets. Most markets in Croatia are open Monday–Saturday 8am–2pm, and many also work Sunday 8–11am. Markets in the holiday resorts also sell souvenirs, and tend to have extended opening hours.

Food items to look out for are *paški sir*, the excellent salty **sheep's milk cheese** from the North Dalmatian island of Pag, as well as the delicious *pršut* **smoked ham**, which is served in thin slices all along the coastline, but particularly in Dalmatia.

Croatian **olive oil** is also highly rated, as are its **truffles**, which are found in the Istrian interior. **Kulen sausage** from Slavonia is a spicy and tasty treat that travels well. On the coast, of course, **fresh fish and seafood** are the highlights, especially the mussels and oysters of places such as Ston and the Lim fjord.

Truffles

Istria is the place to be for truffle lovers. The region's interior is one of Europe's most productive regions for truffle hunting. One of the best places to purchase truffle products is Zigante Tartufi, www.zigantetartufi.com. This retail group, which stakes claim to having found the world's biggest truffle, sells its white truffles, black truffles, truffle oil and truffled sheep's milk cheese throughout Istria. They have branches at Gradiziol 8 in Motovun (tel: 052-681 668), J.B. Tita 12 in Buje (tel: 052-772 125), Trg Fontana in Buzet (tel: 052-663 340), Gorjan 5 in Grožnjan (tel: 052-776 099) and Livade 7 in Livade, where an excellent restaurant serves truffle dishes (tel: 052-664 030).

Croatia is also gaining a reputation for its **wines**, with a multitude of varieties available. Istria and Dalmatia produce the best known and most highly regarded wines, but family-run and larger vineyards can be found all over the country. Good wine can be expensive but the house wines are mostly very drinkable and good value.

Truffles for sale

Prošek, a sweet wine, is delicious served with ice and lemon as an aperitif or with desserts. Many Croatians swear by the health-giving powers of the various fruit and herb brandies *(rakija)* that are often also offered before a meal. **Local beers** (Karlovačko and Ožujsko) are popular too; they are every bit as good as more recognised international brands and considerably cheaper.

Jewellery and Clothes

Items of jewellery, especially **silver pieces and necklaces** made from Adriatic coral, can be found in all of the coastal resorts in summer, sold from small shops or temporary stalls. The jewellery is often made in the outlying villages. Croatia claims to be the original home of the tie, and **handmade silk neckties** *(kravata)* are also popular, as is **lace** from the island of Pag, where the local women have made it by hand for centuries. From Rijeka comes the distinctive traditional *morčić* jewellery.

Designer fashion can be found in Zagreb and Dubrovnik. In Croatia's second city, Split, clothes shopping is a joy. Diocletian's Palace is a dramatic setting for retail therapy in the many small shops in and around the palace. The citizens of Split are among the best dressed people in the country; though prices are not cheap, quality is high, with bespoke items still good value.

Arts and Crafts

Most tourists encounter Croatia's arts and crafts in the coastal resorts in the form of skyline depictions of the historic sights. More interesting are the individual paintings and artworks found in small shops in towns such as Grožnjan and Rovinj.

Where to Shop

Zagreb has a multitude of shops selling the latest fashions and designer clothes and a number of modern malls. The heart of the action is on the grand thoroughfare of Ilica and its surrounding streets. Gharani Štrok Boutique

Art gallery in Grožnjan

(Dežmanova Prolaz 5; tel: 01-484 6152) stocks clothes, shoes and jewellery, and Croata outlets, specialising in Croatian ties, can be found all over Croatia, at airports and major shopping centres.

Lavender, a product of Hvar

One of the best places to purchase Croatian wines, *rakija*, olive oil and truffle products is Vinoteka Bornstein (Kaptol 19; tel: 01-481 2363), located in a large brick cellar close to the cathedral.

For an extensive choice of English-language books, call at Algoritam (Ljudevita Gaja 1) just off the main square.

Shopping centres in the capital include Centar Kaptol (Nova Ves 17), Importanne (Trg Ante Starčevića 7) and Mercatone (Gospodarska 5).

In **Split**, Diocletian's Palace is *the* place to shop, where a number of small domestic designers and international names have their outlets. At the western end of the palace is the shining Marmontova that sweeps seawards in a flashy array of European high street stores and trendy boutiques. Shopping is at its busiest during early evening when the local smart set is out to see and be seen. Split also has its first town centre shopping mall in the Brodarica area near Hotel Atrium and many more just outside the centre, with a huge one springing up near the motorway exit.

In **Dubrovnik**, by the Ploče Gate, Maria Boutique sells international designer labels such as Givenchy and Stella McCartney. There are several small, select wine stores, one of the best being Dubrovačka Kuća (Svetog Dominika; tel:

020-322 092), also close to Ploče Gate, and which has an art gallery selling tasteful paintings by local artists.

In **Istria**, Poreč's charming Ulica Decumanus, where Venetian villas brim with tourist shops, is a good place to look for souvenirs.

Further north, **Rovinj**'s Ulica Grisia is a pretty street given over to small arts and crafts shops. Arguably the best place to purchase original art in Croatia is in the Istrian hill town of **Grožnjan**, a government-sponsored community of artists.

Trogir is the home of Gena (www.gena.hr), which makes traditional handmade suits for the smart man in the street as well as Placido Domingo, Goran Ivanišević and Barack Obama.

ENTERTAINMENT

In the summer months, the Croatian coastline is lively, with smart clubs and stylish cocktail bars vying for trade with the more rustic bars and the omnipresent **summer festivals**. On the coast, things quieten down a bit and many venues close in the winter and often in spring and autumn. Summer can be quiet in inland cities such as Zagreb and Osijek, when most locals escape to the coast.

In **Zagreb** the choice is varied, with live band venues such as Tvornica Kulture, smart DJ clubs like Best, super-discos along the lines of Shamballa and Aquarius, and prestige jazz haunts like BP Club, all a tram ride or walk from the centre.

Outside the capital, other notable bars and clubs include Monvi Center in the

Night on the tiles

Outdoor nightlife begins in April and culminates in July and August, when festivals offer outdoor cultural entertainment. Makarska, on the mainland, and Novalja on Pag offer most fun for the young.

The Moreška is Croatia's traditional sword dance

resort area of **Rovinj**, and Valentino (Santa Croce 28), a fashionable cocktail bar with a waterside terrace. In **Rijeka** look out for Terminal Club in the harbour complex, a slick club with fantastic views.

In **Dubrovnik**, Jazz Caffè Troubadour (Bunićeva Poljana 2) is a famous jazz bar in the old town. Culture Club Revelin brings top DJs to its atmospheric club within the Revelin fort, and offers fantastic views from its roof terrace.

In **Split**, nightlife centres on the Diocletian Palace until 11ish, with clubs such as Hemingway, by the Poljud football stadium, and a clutch around Bačvice, taking over after that. **Zadar**, meanwhile, buzzes with bars and clubs such as The Garden, Arsenal, Shine and Zoilo.

On the islands, **Hvar town** attracts clubbers to Hula Hula, Kiva and Carpe Diem. Pag, meanwhile, has turned itself into the Ibiza of the Adriatic with its giant clubs on Zrće beach in Novalja.

Cultural Performances

There is an extensive cultural programme of theatre, opera and classical music in Zagreb and, to a lesser extent, in the cities of Split, Dubrovnik, Rijeka, Pula, Osijek and Varaždin. In July and August, almost every settlement of any size on the coast has a summer festival. In Dalmatia, you'll hear local folk singing, klapa, everywhere but particularly in Omiš, the site of the annual **Klapa Festival**. Korčula is the birthplace of Croatia's traditional sword dance, the **Moreška**, and performances are held in the outdoor theatre in Korčula Town in high season. The most important Moreška of the year is performed on 27 July on the feast of St Theodore. Contact local tourist offices for more information and tickets.

CROATIA FOR CHILDREN

In Zagreb, the parks make a good escape for younger travellers. Things are better on the coast, though, where the big resorts have plenty to keep children occupied. The larger hotels have **children's clubs**, especially in Poreč.

The waters of the coast are suitable for children, though look out for rocks and sea urchins. Most beaches are pebbly, so some children might prefer to wear swimming shoes. The **Falconry Centre** (www.sokolarskicentar.com) and **Etnoland** (www.dalmati.com), both near Šibenik, are very child friendly. In June 2014, Croatia opened its first dedicated waterpark, Istralandia, which is near Novigrad in Istria.

Kids love the coast

Calendar of Events

Croatia's cultural scene has received a huge boost since independence, with many old festivals resurrected and others given a new lease of life.

January/February Rijeka Carnival: Croatia's third largest city wakes up from its winter slumber in the days preceding Lent.

February Feast of St Blaise, Dubrovnik: gunpowder, religious processions and marching bands for the feast day of Dubrovnik's patron saint.

Easter Celebrated throughout the country: Vodice, near Šibenik, has almost a week-long celebration of Easter with a number of pageants.

Early June Cest is d'Best, Zagreb: street festival with outdoor performances, sports and events around the capital's main square.

Late June–early July The International Children's Festival, Šibenik: a mixture of ballet, art and performances by children's theatre groups.

Late July Pula Film Festival: there can be few better settings in the world for a film festival than the ancient Roman amphitheatre.

Early July–mid-August Musical Evenings in St Donat's (*Glazbene večeri u Sv. Donatu*), Zadar: the acoustics of this medieval church are perfect for grand classical performances.

Mid July–late August Dubrovnik Summer Festival (*Dubrovačke Ljetne Igre*): the festival is rapidly establishing a name for itself as one of Europe's top festivals; tickets are limited, but well worth the effort.

July and August The Summer of Split (*Splitsko Ljeto*): a solid programme of cultural events; many of the performances are in and around Diocletian's Palace. The Summer Events on the Island of Krk: cultural action focuses on Krk Town's old town. Istrian Musical and Cultural Summer: Poreč, Umag, Rovinj, Pula and Grožnjan host cultural events and concerts, as do most towns along the Dalmatian coast.

Late September–early October Varaždin Baroque Evenings (*Varaždinske Barokne Večeri*): opera and baroque ensembles.

6 December St Nicholas Day, Komiža on Vis island: In a tradition that dates back many years, local fishermen organise a procession and burn an old wooden boat in honour of the patron saint of sailors.

24–25 December Christmas festivities throughout the country.

EATING OUT

Croatia's reputation as a destination for food and drink grows every year. Perhaps the ultimate compliment is that many discerning Italians make the journey over the Adriatic every summer in search of some of the best-value seafood in Europe and also the excellent wines that the country produces.

The best seafood restaurants are located along the Adriatic coast, but the cuisine of Slavonia also has its merits, with good river fish and meat dishes that take their influences from Hungary rather than Italy. Zagreb has the greatest choice of restaurants in the country with the cuisine of many nations represented.

When to Eat

In the summer season, most restaurants are open all day, though what is on offer often varies depending on the availability of seafood. Traditionally Croatians are early risers, taking a stiff shot of coffee to kick-start the day, perhaps along with a pastry snack. Lunch is normally taken around noon to 2pm, though this can vary along the coast, where a more Mediterranean lifestyle means later lunches and siestas. Dinner is usually eaten later than in most Western European countries, with restaurants serving food until 10pm or even later.

Out of season, many restaurants, even in the bigger towns, take a week or two off, or sometimes a couple of months. In the smaller

> **Cheap eats**
>
> Eating out is less common among Croatians than in many other European countries – except on special occasions – but you will find locals eating in pizzerias, which are good value and serve excellent pizza.

coastal resorts many close down completely.

What to Eat

There is a great deal of regional variation in Croatia, with seafood the obvious highlight along the coast. In Istria, the Italian influence is strong, whereas in Dalmatia, fish and meat tend to be served with little in the way of sauces. Inland, meat specialities come to the fore and richer Austrian and Hungarian cooking styles prevail. One common thread is quality, with an emphasis on organic produce and freshness. Fish is usually cooked and eaten on the day it is caught, and all towns

Pag's famous cheese goes well with pršut air-dried ham

and villages have a farmers' market. The fast-food culture and product homogeneity that are found in many other European Union countries have yet to descend on the country.

Starters

A common starter in restaurants all over the country is a plate of ham and cheese served with bread. Usually it is the smoked ham known as *pršut*, which is produced in Istria; at its best it is every bit as good as Spain's Serrano ham and Italy's *prosciutto*. The most renowned cheese is *paški sir*, a salty sheep's milk cheese produced on the island of Pag. You can ask for a plate of freshly sliced tomatoes as an accompaniment.

Seafood starters are also good. Highlights include *salata od hobotnice* (octopus salad with olive oil), *lignje* (squid) or the more expensive *salata od jastoga* (pieces of lobster marinated in herbs and olive oil). In Slavonia and inland, hearty soups are also common – look out for *fiš paprikaš* from Slavonia, a spicy stew of river fish such as pike, catfish and carp, and *fažol*, a hearty peasant bean stew from Istria. Mushrooms are also used a lot, notably in Istria, which is also the centre of the truffle industry (see page 88).

Fish and Seafood

Croatia's range of seafood is extensive. There are numerous highlights, but one inexpensive and unfussy dish that sustains many travellers is seafood risotto, which is both tasty and filling. Croatians like to let their seafood speak for itself, and there are few complicated French-style sauces here. Most dishes come na *žaru* (grilled) or *pećena* (roasted). Most fish is sold by weight and at the top restaurants it will be brought out for you to inspect first. Among the bountiful stock in the Adriatic are list (sole), *kovač* (John Dory) and *trilja* (red mullet).

Shellfish are also very popular and of high quality, especially around the *Pelješac* peninsula and the town of Ston. Look out for huge *ostrige* (oysters) and *dagnje* (mussels), the latter sometimes coming with a *buzara* sauce. It's reminiscent of *moules marinières* with garlic and white wine, but with a few tomatoes added. *Jastog* (lobster) is expensive compared with other options, but still very good value. The *škampi* (prawns) are often served whole, simply grilled or in a *buzara* sauce.

Meat

In the resorts, meat dishes may be limited to grilled beef and pork, but it's not too hard to find delicious spit-roasted

Shellfish in Istria

meat, usually chicken, veal, beef or lamb, baked with potatoes under a metal bell *(peka)* in hot embers. Between the coast and Zagreb the hills are dotted with small restaurants that special-ise in spit-roasted lamb and pork. You can tell which places are open by the pigs and lambs slowly turning over the hot coals outside. This is usually served unadorned and accompanied by bread, potatoes, and a simple salad.

In terms of fast food, the ubiquitous *ćevapčići* is much beloved of many Croats, especially the younger genera-tions. These spicy rissoles are succulent and tasty, and usu-ally come with a salad and bread, making a quick, filling lunch option.

The Austrian influence comes through in the Zagorje region north of the capital, where schnitzels are omnipresent on menus. Zagreb even has its own version, the *zagrebački odrezak*, which comes stuffed with cheese and ham. In Slavonia, to the east of the capital, the Hungarian influences bring in paprika and hearty stews such as *gulaš*. A highlight here is the fine *kulen* sausage, a large and spicy affair not dissimilar to Spanish chorizo, which is eaten on its own with bread and used in stews.

Desserts

Ice cream *(sladoled)* is superb in Croatia, rivalling Italian *gelati* in its taste and quality. No hot Adriatic summer's day would be complete without at least one, preferably taken before or after dinner along the waterfront.

Croatian desserts do not stop at ice cream. From the town of Samobor comes *kremšnita*, a creamy and delicate custard cake. *Voćna salata* (fruit salad) is a healthy option, and less so are the common *štrudl* (strudel) and *torta* (gateau).

Desserts tend to get more calorific as you head inland, again thanks to the influences of Austria and Hungary. *Palačinke* (pancakes) come laden with cream, nuts and seasonal fruits, although, along the coast, fillings are generally simpler. For the majority of Croatians, though, dessert is usually just a strong cup of coffee, perhaps followed by an ice cream on a postprandial stroll around town.

A taste of Turkey

Though not as pronounced as in some of the other Balkan countries, Turkish influences are evident, particularly in indigenous fast food such as meat kebabs and *burek* (cheese or meat baked in filo pastry). Among the desserts, you will also find *baklava*, filo pastry smothered in honey and nuts. Turkish coffee, drunk very strong in tiny cups, is popular.

Croatian Wine

Croatia produces a massive array of wines of varying quality, from simple table white wines that go with fish dishes, to excellent reds that stand their ground against many wines from France and Italy. To cut costs, Croatians like to drive

Kremšnita, a delicious custard cream dessert from Samobor

out to the vineyards and stock up on supplies. Istria and the Samobor Hills near Zagreb are packed with small-scale producers selling direct to customers.

Red Wines. Dingač from the Pelješac peninsula in southern Dalmatia is regarded as the king of Croatian wines. This robust 14 percent wine goes well with all meat dishes and is also very good on its own, although it can be expensive. Pelješac is also home to the considerably cheaper red Plavac, more often than not served as table wine, though certain vintages can also stand on their own. Postup is another Pelješac wine that has been compared to American Zinfandel.

Further north in Dalmatia, Šibenik produces its own Plavina and Babić wines, as well as an acceptable rosé. Neighbouring Primošten produces its own excellent Babić. Although most production in Istria is of white wine, Teran is a passable red, though it can be overloaded with tannin.

Biska, a mistletoe-based spirit, with local produce in Istria

White Wines. In the north, more than 70 percent of Istria's production is white wine. Look out for Muscatel and Malvazija. In southern Dalmatia, tucked on the end of the Pelješac peninsula, is the island of Korčula, which is renowned for its Pošip and the especially good Grk, both varieties of white.

It is thought that wine was first produced in Croatia by the Greeks on the island of Vis. Today Vis has myriad vineyards that specialise in Viški Plavac (red) and Vugava (white), with many small scale operations. Arguably the best of all the island wines is Vrbnička Žlahtina. From the vine-covered slopes around Vrbnik, in the north of the Kvarner Gulf island of Krk, this straw-yellow wine is superb and goes particularly well with the local fish dishes; it is also good for drinking on its own on steamy summer nights. A good dessert wine is Prošek, which is the perfect accompaniment to the very sweet desserts and often drunk as an aperitif with ice and lemon.

It is common for locals to dilute their wine with a little water (called a *bevanda*) or add a touch of sparkling mineral water (*gemišt*), with Vrbnička Žlahtina working well in both cases. Connoisseurs may be distressed to see Croatians pouring orange juice into their glasses of red wine, but it actually makes for a very refreshing drink when the temperature rises.

Away from the coast, Slavonia produces some excellent white wines; like the local food, these are very distinctive in character. Two to look out for are Graševina and also Kutjevo Chardonnay, which complement the spicy fish dishes of the region.

Other Drinks

Beer (*pivo*) is a popular drink, especially in summer. Foreign import brands are becoming increasingly widespread, but thankfully, there is a good range of domestically owned and produced beers. The best of them all, and commonly available, is Karlovačko, from Karlovac, which has a clean, crisp flavour and a pleasant aftertaste. Its biggest rival is Ošujsko from Zagreb, a heavier tasting lager beer that rewards repeated tastings.

In Slavonia you'll find the less well-known Ozječko, which is an excellent lager. Most visitors tend to avoid Istria's Favorit after their first sample, and with good reason, as it has a slightly metallic flavour and a poor aftertaste.

Domestic spirits are hugely popular and found in most bars and restaurants. They include the fiery grappa digestif, which can be dynamite, especially if it is home made. *Šljivovica* (plum brandy) is a good digestif, but it can also have quite a kick. Beware of getting drawn into a drinking competition on this spirit as Croatians seem to be able to handle it like Russians do vodka, while tourists generally end up collapsing.

Other domestic spirits include maraschino, a cherry liqueur from Zadar, and *biska*, a mistletoe-based aperitif produced in inland Istria.

TO HELP YOU ORDER

Could we have a table for…? **Imate li stol za…?**
Please could you bring…? **Molim vas donesite…?**
The bill, please **Račun molim**
menu **jelovnik**

bread **kruh**	salad **salata**
butter **maslac**	salt **sol**
coffee **kava**	sugar **šećer**
dessert **desert**	tea **čaj**
fish **riba**	with milk **s mlijekom**
fruit **voće**	with lemon **s limunom**
ice cream **sladoled**	with rum **s rumom**
meat **meso**	wine **vino**
milk **mlijeko**	white **bijelo**
pepper **papar**	red **crno**
rice **riža**	rosé **roze**

MENU READER

bakalar cod	**ispod peke** baked under a cast-iron bell
banana banana	
biftek beefsteak	**jabuka** apple
ćevapčići spicy rissoles	**jagoda** strawberry
crna kava black coffee	**jaje** egg
dagnje mussels	**janje na ražnju** lamb on the spit
gljive mushrooms	
goveđi beef	**jastog** lobster
grah beans	**juha** soup
gulaš goulash	**kamenica/ostriga** oyster
hladno pečenje cold meat	**kobasica** sausage
	kolač cake
hobotnica octopus	**krastavac** cucumber

krumpir potato
kulen Slavonian sausage
lignje squid
ljuskar shellfish
luk onion
marmelada jam
masline olives
med honey
mineralna voda mineral
  water
naranča orange
omlet sa šunkom ham
  omelette
palačinke pancakes
pečeni odojak na ražnju
  roast suckling pig on
  the spit
pile chicken
pivo beer
pršut Parma ham

purica turkey
rakija brandy
rižot risotto
salata salad
sir cheese
škampi prawns
slag whipped cream
šljivovica plum brandy
stolno vino table wine
šunka ham
sirova raw
kuhana cooked
dimljena smoked
svinjski kotleti pork chops
tartufe truffle
teleći odrezak veal cutlet
voćna salata fruit salad
voćni sok fruit juice
zelena paprika green
  pepper

Restaurant Culture

There are several kinds of restaurant in Croatia. The first is the formal *restoran*, which are plentiful in the big resorts and cities and usually offer international food. More authentic and more likely to provide regional specialities is a *konoba* (inn), a small family-run restaurant. These often offer dishes of the day and may not even run to a standard menu; the choice varies depending on what is freshest and cheapest at the morning market. The last category is roadside establishments, often called *gostionica*, serving succulent spit-roasted pork and lamb with bread and simple salads.

PLACES TO EAT

We have used the following symbols to give an idea of the price for a three-course meal for two people, including a bottle of house wine but excluding tip:

$$$$ over 440kn $$ 220–330kn
$$$ 330–440kn $ under 220kn

CENTRAL AND EASTERN CROATIA

ZAGREB

Baltazar $$$ *Nova Ves 4, 10000 Zagreb, tel: 01-466 6999, www. restoran-baltazar.hr.* Open Mon–Sat 12pm–12am, Sun 12–5pm. Barbecued meats served in a rustic dining room in winter and in a courtyard garden in summer. Situated in Gornji Grad, close to the cathedral.

Pod Gričkim Topom $$$ *Zakmardijeve Stube 5, 10000 Zagreb, tel: 01-483 3607, www.restoran-pod-grickim-topom.hr.* Open Mon–Sat 11am–12am. Up in Gornji Grad, near the funicular station, this informal restaurant serves up Dalmatian meat and fish dishes, and also offers fantastic views over the city. Closed Sun evening.

Vinodol $$$ *Nikole Tesle 10, 10000 Zagreb, tel: 01-481 1427, www. vinodol-zg.hr.* Open daily 10am–12am. Vaulted ceilings keep things cosy on cold days in this Donji Grad restaurant, which spills out into a huge courtyard terrace on warmer days. Veal cooked slowly under a peka is one of the specialities, along with veal served with a cheese crust, Zagreb style.

OSIJEK

Slavonska Kuća $$ *Kamila Firingera 26, 31000 Osijek, tel: 031-369 955, www.slavonskakuca.com.* Open daily for lunch and dinner. A traditional Slavonian restaurant in the historic Tvrđa, renowned for its spicy fish stew.

VARAŽDIN

Pivnica Raj $ *Ivana Gundulića 11, 42000 Varaždin, tel: 042-648 114*. Open daily for dinner and until 1am on Saturdays. This lively beer hall has a hearty and extensive meat-based menu.

ISTRIA

POREČ

Gourmet Restaurant $$ *Eufrazijeva 26, 52440 Poreč, tel: 052-452 742*. This traditional Italian-style pizzeria serves up pasta and pizza dishes on a lively terrace in one of Poreč's most beautiful squares.

Pizzeria Dali $ *Istarskog razvoda 11, 52440 Poreč, tel: 052-452 666*. Wood-fired pizzas and pasta dishes are served in this small and traditional restaurant in the heart of town.

PULA

Pivnica Tomaso $ *Zagrebačka 13, 52100 Pula, tel: 052-216 027*. Open Mon–Sat 8am–6pm. Small pizzeria in the centre, serving good-value pizzas and pasta dishes.

Scaletta $$$$ *Flavijevska 26, 52100 Pula, tel: 052-541 599, www. hotel-scaletta.com*. Fine-dining restaurant in the Scaletta Hotel close to the amphitheatre, with fish and meat specialities. Try the scampi soup, gnocchi with gorgonzola and excellent fish platter. It also serves lobster for special occasions.

ROVINJ

Enoteca Al Gastaldo $$ *Iza Kasarne 14, 52210 Rovinj, tel: 052-814 109*. Open daily for lunch and dinner. This cosy restaurant serves Italian and Istrian dishes. Try the beefsteak with truffles.

Giannino $$ *Augusto Ferrija, 38, 52210 Rovinj, tel: 052-813 402*. Open daily for lunch and dinner. Giannino serves first-rate fish. It is located in a secluded street away from the main tourist area.

THE KVARNER GULF

OPATIJA

Le Mandrać $$$ *Obala Frana Supila 10, Volosko, 51410 Opatija, tel: 051-701 357, www.lemandrac.com.* Bosnian chef Deniz Zembo does sublime things with seafood at this new-wave Croatian restaurant, situated at the end of the Lungomare promenade beside the fishing harbour at Volosko.

THE ISLANDS

Konoba Rab $$$ *Kneza Branimira 3, 51280 Rab, tel: 051-725 666.* In the old town, this old-fashioned restaurant serves tasty meat and fish in a cosy dining room. Try *rabska torta* (Rab cake, a local speciality made from almonds) for dessert.

Nada $$$ *Ulica Glavača 22, 51516 Vrbnik, Krk, tel: 051-857 065, www.nada-vrbnik.hr.* Open Mar–Oct daily. This highly regarded restaurant serves local meat and fish specialities on a large terrace in the old town. Be sure to try the local Žlahtina white wine, which you can also buy here in presentation boxes to take home.

Pizzeria Draga $$ *Braće Vidulića 77, 51550 Mali Lošinj, tel: 051-231 132.* Lošinj's favourite pizzeria serves pizza, pasta and salads on a large covered terrace just one block back from the harbour.

DALMATIA

DUBROVNIK

Lokanda Peskarija $ *Na Ponti bb, 20000 Dubrovnik, tel: 020-324 750, www.mea-culpa.hr.* Situated next to the covered fish market in an atmospheric setting overlooking the old harbour, this informal restaurant serves excellent seafood. Very popular with locals, so reservations are essential for dinner.

Orhan $$$ *Od Tabakarije 1, 20000 Dubrovnik, tel: 020-414 183, www.restaurant-orhan.com.* Just outside the city walls, close to

Pile Gate, Orhan serves up Dalmatian seafood dishes at outdoor tables overlooking the sea.

Sesame $$ *Dante Alighieria bb, 20000 Dubrovnik, tel: 020-412 910*, www.sesame.hr. Open daily for lunch and dinner. This taverna near the Pile gate serves local specialities such as seafood risotto.

MALI STON

Kapetenova Kuča $$$ *20234 Mali Ston, tel: 020-754 555*, www. ostrea.hr. Open daily for lunch and dinner. This is one of Croatia's top restaurants specialising in oysters and seafood. Try to save room for pudding too, as the gateaux are delicious. Booking ahead recommended.

MAKARSKA

Stari Mlin $$$ *Prvosvibanjska 43, 21300 Makarska, tel: 021-611 509*. Colourful paintings, candles and incense set the mood in this old stone building with a vine-covered terrace. The menu is rather special – Dalmatian seafood dishes plus select Thai specialities.

ŠIBENIK

Pelegrini $$$ *Jurja Dalmatinca 1, 22000 Šibenik, tel: 022-213 701*, www.pelegrini.hr. Open daily for lunch and dinner June–Oct; closed Mon Apr–May; Thur–Sat (Sun lunch only) Nov–Mar; closed Jan. A wonderfully located restaurant with outdoor and some indoor tables that have stunning views of the cathedral and over the estuary. Domestic cuisine with an international touch.

SPLIT

Galija $$ *Tončićeva 12, 21000 Split, tel: 021-347 932*. This cosy pizzeria serves some of the city's best pizzas just outside Diocletian's Palace.

Kod Jože $$ *Sredmanuška 4, 21000 Split, tel: 021-347 397*. All a *konoba* should have: flagstone floor, wooden furniture, great barbecued fish and an endless supply of local wine served by candlelight.

THE ISLANDS

Adio Mare $$ *Marko Polo 2, 20260 Korčula, tel: 020-711 253*. Open Apr–Oct for dinner only. A real gem hidden in a narrow side street in the old town. Serves typical Dalmatian meat and fish dishes.

Macondo $$$$ *Groda, 21450 Hvar, tel: 021-742 850*. Open Apr–Oct daily for lunch and dinner. One of Hvar's best restaurants, situated in a narrow street set back from the main square.

Mali Raj $$$ *Put Zlatnog rata, 21420 Bol, Brač, tel: 021-635 282*. Open May–Oct daily for lunch and dinner. Right by the main beach, excellent fish and meat in a lovely setting.

Villa Kaliopa $$$$ *V. Nazora 32. 21480 Vis, tel: 021-711 755*. Open in summer daily for dinner. Romantic setting in the garden of a Renaissance villa. Classic Dalmatian meat and fish with a menu that changes according to what's fresh caught on the day.

TROGIR

Restoran Fontana $$ *Obrov 1, 21220 Trogir, tel: 021-884 811*, www.fontana-commerce-htnet.hr. Open daily for lunch and dinner. Fresh fish and pizza.

ZADAR

Bife More $$ *Brne Kanarutica 3, Zadar*. It's easy to miss this tiny restaurant in a narrow side street, but it's worth looking out for it if you want nicely grilled squid and prawns for relatively little money.

Foša $$ *Kralja Dimitra Zvonimira 2, 23000 Zadar, tel: 023-314 421*, www.fosa.hr. Open daily for lunch and dinner. Traditional fish restaurant located in the former customs house. Enjoy a fish platter or spaghetti with clams.

A–Z TRAVEL TIPS

A Summary of Practical Information

A Accommodation ...112
   Airports 113
B Bicycle Rental 114
   Budgeting for
      Your Trip 114
C Camping 115
   Car Hire 115
   Climate 116
   Crime and Safety...116
D Driving............117
E Electricity..........118
   Embassies and
      Consulates 119
   Emergencies.......119
G Gay and Lesbian
      Travellers.........119
   Getting There......119
   Guides and Tours...120
H Health and
      Medical Care 121

L Language 121
M Money 123
O Opening Times.....124
P Police 125
   Post Offices 125
   Public Holidays.....126
T Telephones 126
   Time Zones 127
   Tipping............127
   Toilets.............127
   Tourist
      Information.......127
   Transport 129
V Visas and Entry
      Requirements ...130
W Websites and
      Internet Access ..131
Y Youth Hostels......132

A

ACCOMMODATION

Hotels, apartments, campsites and private accommodation in Croatia are all graded by the government and receive one to five stars. Standards in four- and five-star establishments are consistently high, but there are greater variations in the lower grades.

Hotels. Croatia offers a wide variety of hotels, from clean and functional resort hotels to luxurious business-oriented establishments and intimate boutique hotels. Hotels in the popular coastal regions fill up quickly for July and August, so book several months in advance. Resorts in high season often demand minimum stays and half-board arrangements, while many close from October to March (see pages 133).

Private accommodation. This ranges from basic rooms to exclusive use of apartments. Book through a travel agent and beware of the feisty ladies who greet tourists off the ferry.

Farmhouses. In Istria, the *Agroturizam* programme offers visitors the opportunity to stay in a family home or a traditional stone farmhouse in the tranquil Istrian hills. Here you can experience a taste of the real Croatia away from the resorts. Further information on the *Agroturizam* programme can be found at www.istra.com, or from the Istria County Tourist Association, tel: 052-452 797.

Lighthouses. One of the more unusual accommodation options in Croatia comes in the form of renovated but still operational lighthouses. Croatian Lighthouses (www.lighthouses-croatia.com) can supply information about stays (and online booking) in one of 11 lighthouses located on headlands and islands in Istria and Dalmatia.

I'd like a single/double room **Ja bih jednokrevetnu sobu/ dvokrevetnu sobu**
with bath/shower **sa banjom/tušem**
How much does it cost per night? **Koliko košta za jednu noć?**

Campsites. Croatia also has a large number of campsites called *autocamps*, most of which have good amenities and numerous recreational facilities (see page 115).

AIRPORTS

Zagreb international airport (ZAG: tel: 01-456 2222, www.zagreb-airport.hr) is 17km (12 miles) south of the capital. Pleso Prijevoz (tel: 01-633 1999, www.plesoprijevoz.hr) operates an efficient shuttle bus between the airport and the city centre. The journey takes 30–45 minutes and costs 30kn. A taxi into town takes around 20 minutes; fares start at about 200kn.

Croatia's other international airports are:

Split (SPU; tel: 021-203 555, www.split-airport.hr) is 24km (14 miles) from the city, journey time 35 minutes; direct buses with Pleso Prijevoz cost 30kn each way.

Dubrovnik (DBV; tel: 020-773 100, www.airport-dubrovnik.hr) is 18km (11 miles) from the city, journey time 20 minutes; direct buses with Atlas cost 35kn each way.

Pula (PUY; tel: 052-530 105, www.airport-pula.hr) is 7km (4 miles) from the city, journey time 10 minutes; shuttle bus to Pula with Fils costs €4 each way.

Rijeka (RJK; tel: 051-841 222, www.rijeka-airport.hr) is 27km (17 miles) from the city, journey time 35 minutes; direct buses with Pleso Prijevoz cost 180kn each way.

Osijek (OSI; tel: 031-514 400, www.osijek-airport.hr) is 3km (1.5 miles) from the city, journey time 10 minutes; transfers cost 25kn each way.

Zadar (ZAD; tel: 023-205 800, www.zadar-airport.hr) is 15km (9 miles) from the city, journey time 15 minutes; transfers with Liburnija cost 25kn each way.

The coastal airports at Pula, Rijeka, Zadar, Split and Dubrovnik are served by regular scheduled and budget flights, with additional routes in summer. Shuttle buses are timed to coincide with flight arrivals and departures.

B

BICYCLE RENTAL

It is relatively easy and cheap to hire a bicycle in Croatia, but congested roads and fast traffic make cycling dangerous in certain areas. The local tourist office is the best source of information about where to hire a bicycle. Many tourist boards now have special cycling routes with maps available.

BUDGETING FOR YOUR TRIP

Compared to most western European destinations, Croatia is still relatively inexpensive.

Accommodation. Hotel prices are often quoted in euros, but you can pay in Croatian *kuna*. A double room with breakfast in a five-star hotel will cost at least 1,200kn, but you can get a comfortable room in a three-star hotel for around 600kn. Most hotels have a scale of prices depending on the season. Private accommodation costs at least 100kn per person per night, plus taxes. All registered providers of accommodation are obliged to charge tourist tax, a nominal amount.

Meals. For many European visitors, the prices in Croatia's most expensive restaurants are surprisingly affordable. A three-course meal for two with wine in a reputable restaurant costs around 400kn. A simple lunchtime snack, such as grilled meat with bread, salad and mineral water, can cost less than 150kn. Look out for special lunchtime menus which are considerably cheaper than the evening equivalent.

Nightlife. Alcoholic drinks in Croatia are reasonably priced, with a half-litre of beer costing around 13kn. The average price for a soft drink or a small bottle of water is about 13kn.

Incidentals. Locally organised day trips start at around 200kn. Charges for museums and attractions vary enormously, with very few free museums to be found. Some will have a nominal charge of about 20kn, while others (Dubrovnik's ramparts, for example) can be as high as 90kn.

C

CAMPING

Croatia has more than 500 campsites that cater for a wide range of holidaymakers, including families and naturists. Many sites offer extensive land- and water-based sporting activities. Most campsites are only open from April to October, some just July and August. Overnight rates can be as little as 45kn for two people.

Approximately 90 percent of the campsites lie along the Adriatic coast and on the surrounding islands. The best-equipped and most highly organised sites are found in the regions of Istria and Kvarner in the north. For those who really want to escape modern-day living, the most memorable sites are in Dalmatia. Koversada in Vrsar, Istria, claims to be the largest naturist campsite in Europe.

For a list of campsites, contact the Croatian Camping Union; Bože Milanovića 20, Poreč; tel: 052-451 324; www.camping.hr.

CAR HIRE

International and local car-hire companies operate throughout Croatia. Drivers must be over 21 years old and have held a valid driving licence for a minimum of two years. A credit card and a current passport or national identity card are also required for car hire.

Basic insurance is included in the price, but it is advisable to purchase Collision Damage Waiver (CDW) and Theft Protection (TP) for the duration of the hire. Accidents must be reported to the police (tel: 112) immediately, otherwise the insurance is void.

I want to rent a car **Želim iznajmiti auto**
tomorrow **sutra**
for one day/one week **na jedan dan/jednu sedmicu**
Please include full insurance **Molim vas uključite kasko osiguranje**

Prices for a weekly economy rental (such as a Fiat Uno) vary widely, but can start at about 2,200kn in mid to high season. **Avis** (tel: 01-467 3603; www.avis.com.hr), **Budget** (tel: 01-480 5688; www.budget.hr), **Dollar Thrifty** (tel: 021-399 000; www.subrosa.hr) and **Sixt** (tel: 01-665 1599; www.sixt.hr) all have online booking facilities. Check car rental websites such as www.carrentals.co.uk for online deals.

CLIMATE

The best time to visit Croatia is during late spring, summer and early autumn when days are sunny and dry. Coastal temperatures regularly reach 30°C (86°F) in August. The Croatian coast is significantly warmer than its interior in winter. In January, temperatures in the east of the country can fall as low as –5°C (23°F) but can be as high as 10°C (50°F) in Istria. Autumn, although mild, can be wet. The temperature chart that follows is for Croatia's capital city, Zagreb.

	J	F	M	A	M	J	J	A	S	O	N	D
min °C	-4	-3	2	5	9	13	15	14	11	7	3	-1
min °F	24	27	36	41	48	55	59	57	52	45	37	30
max °C	3	6	11	16	21	24	27	26	23	16	8	5
max °F	37	43	52	61	70	75	81	79	73	61	46	41

CRIME AND SAFETY

Crime rates in Croatia are lower than those in many European countries and crimes against tourists are rare. However, as in any other country, visitors should use their common sense: carry personal belongings securely; do not leave valuables in unattended vehicles or on the beach; don't stop if someone tries to flag you down on the roadside, and avoid walking alone at night in poorly lit areas. If you are a victim of crime, call the emergency services, tel: 112. Uncleared land mines pose a risk only in isolated areas and are usually signed. However, do not stray from roads, public areas or established paths without a qualified guide.

D

DRIVING

As in the rest of Continental Europe, drive on the right in Croatia. Motorways run between Zagreb and along much of the coast, but traffic jams caused by slow-moving vehicles and frequent accidents remain a common problem on single lane roads and in hotspots on the motorways during peak summer weekends.

Road conditions. Croatia's motorway network has a toll system and the roads are in a good condition. Road surfaces on many other main routes are also good, with frequent passing places.

Rules and regulations. To drive your own vehicle in Croatia you will need a valid driving licence, registration documents and Green Card insurance. Speed limits are 50kmh (30mph) in residential areas, 80kmh (50mph) outside residential areas, 100kmh (60mph) on highways and 130kmhr (80mph) on motorways. With limited exceptions, when 0.5 percent is permissible, there is zero tolerance on alcohol for drivers. It is compulsory to wear seat belts and mobile phones should not be used while driving. Headlights should be switched on at all times while driving during the daylight saving period (October to March). Check the detailed regulations for requirements for snow chains, hazard warnings, spare bulbs and safety equipment.

autobusna stanica bus stop
križanje crossroads/crossing
opasan zavoj/opasan krivina dangerous bend/
   dangerous curve
opasnost danger
parkiranje dozvoljeno/zabranjeno parkiranje parking
   permitted/no parking
pažnja, radovi men working
pješaci pedestrians

slijepa ulica no through road (dead end)
stani halt
stop stop
strm uspon steep hill
vozi na desnoj/lijevoj strani drive on the right/left
vozi oprezno drive with care
zabranjen ulaz no entry
zaobilaznica detour
Are we on the right road for...? **Je li ovo cesta za...?**
Fill the tank, please, with... **Napunite spremnik goriva, molim, sa...**
My car's broken down. **Auto mi se pokvarilo.**
There's been an accident. **Dogodila se prometna nesreća.**

The police must be informed immediately about traffic accidents (tel: 112). Violations like speeding can incur an on-the-spot fine.

Parking. Car parks, often located just outside the pedestrianised old towns, cost 5–20kn an hour. Fees are often charged 24 hours a day, seven days a week. In some places the arrival of a tow-away truck can be very swift.

If you need help. The Croatian Automobile Club (Hrvatski Autoklub – hak) provides emergency breakdown assistance (tel: 987, www.hak.hr). Calls should be prefixed 01 if made from a mobile telephone.

Road signs. Croatian road signs generally use internationally recognised pictographs.

E

ELECTRICITY

The standard current is 220-volt, 50Hz. Plugs have two round pins.

EMBASSIES AND CONSULATES

Zagreb is the main diplomatic base and a number of countries have embassy representatives in Split.

Australia: Centar Kaptol, Nova Ves 11/3; tel: 01-489 1200; www.croatia.embassy.gov.au

Canada: Prilaz Đure Deželića 4; tel: 01-488 1200; www.canadainternational.gc.ca.

Ireland: Miramarska 23; tel: 01-631 0025; www.dfa.ie.

South Africa: Agrikor dd, Trg Draženа Petrovića 3; tel: 01-489 4111; www.dfa.gov.za.

UK: Ivana Lučića 4; tel: 01-600 9100; http://ukincroatia.fco.gov.uk

US: Thomasa Jeffersona 2; tel: 01-661 2200; http://zagreb.usembassy.gov.

Most embassies and consulates are open Mon–Fri 8 or 9am–4 or 5pm, and close for an hour at lunchtime.

EMERGENCIES

Dial 112 for all emergency services.

G

GAY AND LESBIAN TRAVELLERS

The main religion in Croatia is Roman Catholic and, following the view of the Church, homosexuality is tolerated, but not encouraged. There is a limited gay scene in cities and resorts such as Zagreb, Dubrovnik, Rovinj and Hvar. See www.travel.gay.hr.

GETTING THERE

Croatia's national airline (www.croatiaairlines.hr) and its partners connect the country with at least 30 other European cities, including London, Paris, Rome, Vienna, Brussels, Zurich and Munich. British Airways (www.ba.com) has direct flights from London Gatwick to Zagreb and Dubrovnik. EasyJet (www.easyjet.com) covers much of the country, with flights from London Gatwick to Zagreb; from London Gatwick, London Stansted and Bristol to Split; and from London Gatwick, London Stansted and Edinburgh to Dubrovnik. Wizzair (www.wizzair.com) flies from London Luton to Split. Jet2 (www.jet2.com) has flights from Belfast, Newcastle, Leeds Bradford, Manchester, Edinburgh, Glasgow, East Midlands, Blackpool and Cork to Split, and from Manchester, Leeds Bradford, Glasgow, Edinburgh and Newcastle to Pula. Flybe (www.flybe.com) flies from Birmingham to Dubrovnik. Ryanair (www.ryanair.com) flies from London Stansted to Pula, Rijeka and Osijek, and also operates flights from London Stansted, East Midlands, Liverpool and Dublin to Zadar. Other options include indirect flights to Zagreb, Dubrovnik, Split, Rijeka, Pula and Zadar via Germany with TUIfly (www.tuifly.com) and Germanwings (www.germanwings.com). Compare flights and find deals with www.skyscanner.net, www.kayak.com and www.momondo.com. Flight times are about 2.5 hours, and air fares vary wildly from season to season, often rising to extortionate heights during the summer if not booked well in advance.

GUIDES AND TOURS

Escorted coach tours are a popular way to see Croatia, as are guided walking tours of cities and towns. Local travel agents and tourist offices can arrange either of these.

One of the biggest operator with branches throughout Croatia is **Atlas** (www.atlas-croatia.com), now part of Adriatica.net. At the other end of the scale, niche operators such as **Secret Dalmatia** (www.secretdalmatia.com), Regent Holidays (www.regent-holidays.co.uk) and **Original Travel** (www.originaltravel.co.uk) are opening up less discovered secrets of Croatia to visitors.

Local travel agencies can provide visitors with information about one-day or longer guided tours and excursions, as well as information on specialist activities such as sailing, shooting, fishing, climbing, horse riding and adventure sports.

H

HEALTH AND MEDICAL CARE

It is safe to drink tap water throughout Croatia, and visitors do not require any inoculations to travel here. The most common health problems experienced by visitors are the result of sunstroke, sunburn and dehydration, sometimes exacerbated by too much alcohol.

During summer insect repellent is recommended, as is the wearing of jelly shoes when swimming in rocky areas, because of spiny sea urchins. Contact with these is painful and requires medical attention.

The UK and many European countries have an agreement with Croatia that offers their citizens free medical care. However, all visitors should take out private travel insurance to cover any unforeseen medical expenses. Local tourist offices have lists of doctors, medical centres, hospitals, dentists and pharmacies (called an apoteka or ljekarna, usually with large green cross).

Where's the nearest (all-night) pharmacy? **Gdje je najbliža apoteka (24-satna)**
I need a doctor/dentist **Trebao bih liječnika/zubara**
hospital **bolnica**
an upset stomach **boli me želudac**
sunburn/a fever **opekotina od sunca/groznica**

L

LANGUAGE

Pronunciation is regular and easy. The accents on letters are important – c is a different letter from č and pronounced very differently, and lj is a 'letter' in its own right. Below are some guidelines where pronunciation of letters differs from English.
a like the 'a' in 'cat'

c like the 'ts' in 'hats'
č like the 'ch' in 'chink'
ć like the 'tch' in 'catch'
dž like the 'j' in 'judge'
e like the 'e' in 'fell'
g like the 'g' in 'golf'
h a guttural sound like the 'ch' in 'loch'
i like the 'ee' in 'yippee'
j like the 'y' in 'yahoo'
k like the 'c' in 'cap'
lj like the 'll' in 'millionaire'
nj like the 'ny' in canyon
o like the 'o' in 'tot'
r always 'rolled'
s like the 's' in 'sing'
š like the 'sh' in 'shine'
u like the 'oo' in 'moo'
z like the 'z' in 'crazy'
ž like the 's' in 'pleasure'

good morning/afternoon/evening **dobro jutro/dan/večer**
goodbye **do viđenja**
please **molim**
thank you **hvala**
Excuse me **oprostite**
yesterday/today/tomorrow **jučer/danas/sutra**
day/week/month/year **dan/tjedan/mjesec/godina**
where/when/how **gdje/kada/kako**
Is this the road to...? **Je li ovo cesta za...?**
how long/how far? **koliko dugo/koliko daleko?**
left/right **lijevo/desno**
cheap/expensive **jeftin/skup**

hot/cold/warm **vruće/hladno/toplo**
old/new **star/nov**
open/closed **otvoreno/zatvoreno**
vacant/occupied **prazan/zauzet**
early/late **rano/kasno**
What does this mean? **Što ovo znači?**
I don't understand **Ne razumijem**
I don't know **Ne znam**
Can you write it down **Možete li mi to zapisati?**
Help me, please **Molim vas pomozite mi**
Get a doctor, quickly! **Trebam doktora brzo!**
Pleased to meet you **Drago mi je**
How are you? **Kako ste?**
Very well thank you, and yourself? **Dobro hvala, a vi?**

Days
Sunday **nedjelja**
Monday **ponedjeljak**
Tuesday **utorak**
Wednesday **srijeda**
Thursday **četvrtak**
Friday **petak**
Saturday **subota**
What day/date is today? **Koji je danas dan/datum?**

MONEY

Currency. The national currency is the *kuna* (abbreviated kn). The *kuna* is divided into 100 *lipa* (lp). Banknotes come in denominations of 5, 10, 20, 50, 100, 200, 500, and 1,000 *kuna* and coins are 1, 2 and 5 *kuna*, 1, 2, 5, 10, 20 and 50 *lipa*. Although Croatia is not yet a member of the eurozone, hotel room prices are often quoted in euros.

Currency exchange. Normal banking hours are Mon–Fri 7am–3pm and Sat 8am–2pm. Currency can also be exchanged in exchange offices, hotels and at any post office counter. You must take your passport.

ATMs. Cashpoints are readily available and debit cards carrying the Maestro, MasterCard, Visa, Cirrus and Plus symbols are widely accepted.

Credit cards. Credit card cash advances can be withdrawn from atms and standard international credit cards are widely accepted, though not in many of the smaller shops, hotels and restaurants.

Traveller's cheques. Euro or US dollar traveller's cheques can be exchanged at any banks and many exchange offices for a commission of up to 2 percent. You must take your passport.

> Can I pay with this credit card? **Primate li kreditne kartice?**
> I want to change some pounds/dollars **Želim promijeniti engleske funte/američke dolare**
> Can you cash a traveller's cheque? **Možete li mi unovčiti putni ček?**
> Where's the nearest bank/currency exchange office? **Gdje je najbliža banka/mjenjačnica?**
> How much is that? **Koliko ovo košta?**

OPENING TIMES

Business hours are generally Mon–Fri 8am–4pm. Banks are open Mon–Fri 7am–3pm and Sat 8am–2pm. Shops and department stores in Croatia usually open Mon–Fri 8am–7pm and Sat 8am–2pm. In the resorts shops often open Mon–Fri 8am–1pm, close for the afternoon and open again in the evening, 5–11pm.

Some larger towns have a 24-hour pharmacy and some have 24-hour grocery shops. Café-bars usually open daily 7am–midnight and most restaurants open from midday to midnight. Internet cafés usually have long opening hours, and are open daily. Museum opening times vary considerably and they are often closed on Monday.

Many Croatian towns and resorts have a fresh food market and a general market. Guide opening times are Mon–Sat 8am–2pm; some also open Sun 8–11am. Markets selling souvenirs often have longer opening hours.

Note that family run businesses and smaller museums may often vary their opening times considerably, according to the season and often at short notice, because of individual circumstances or their judgement of the likelihood of tourist business.

P

POLICE

Croatian police wear dark blue uniforms and are generally helpful and friendly; some speak English.

Anyone involved in a road traffic accident is legally required to report it to the police and not to move the vehicle unless it is causing danger or an obstruction. In the case of emergency, tel: **112**.

Where's the nearest police station? **Gdje je najbliža policijska stanica?**
I've lost my wallet/bag/passport **Izgubio sam novčanik/torbu/putovnicu**

POST OFFICES

Post offices are identifiable by the words Hrvatska Pošta and their yellow signs. Hrvatska Pošta (www.posta.hr) provides a wide variety of services from selling stamps and exchanging foreign currency to sending faxes. Some towns have separate post offices for handling large parcels. Post offices in cities and large towns are open Mon–Sat 7am–8pm and Sun 7am–2pm. In smaller towns the post office may close at noon while those in tourist resorts operate a split shift opening Mon–Sat 7am–1pm and Mon–Fri 5 or 7–9pm. Letterboxes are yellow and have a Hrvatska Pošta sign.

PUBLIC HOLIDAYS

The following is a list of the national holidays in Croatia:

1 January **Nova Godina** New Year's Day

6 January **Sveta tri kralja** Epiphany

1 May **Međunarodni Praznik Rada** Labour Day

22 June **Dan antifašističke borbe** Anti-Fascist Resistance Day

25 June **Dan Državnosti** Croatian National Day

5 August **Dan Pobjede i Dan Domovinske Zahvalnosti** Victory Day and National Thanksgiving Day

15 August **Velika Gospa** Feast of the Assumption

8 October **Dan Nezavisnosti** Independence Day

1 November **Dan Svih Svetih** All Saints' Day

25–6 December **Božićni blagdani** Christmas Holidays

Movable dates:

Uskrs Easter

Corpus Christi Corpus Christi

T

TELEPHONES

Croatia's country code is 385. When calling from overseas the initial 0 in the local area code should not be dialled. Mobile phone numbers begin 09 and all the digits must be dialled.

Mobile phone coverage is extensive throughout the country, but with patchy coverage in some of the mountainous hinterland. Call and data charges are the same as in other EU countries, but for longer stays you might want to buy a local SIM card. While 4G is spreading around the country, there are still inland areas where there is not even 3G and you won't be able to receive data.

> Can you get me this number? **Možete li molim vas nazvati ovaj broj?**
> Reverse charge (collect) **naplatite osobi koju zovem**
> Personal call **osobni poziv**

TIME ZONES

Croatia operates GMT+1 from November to March, and is one hour ahead of the UK, six hours ahead of New York, one hour behind Johannesburg, nine hours behind Sydney and 11 hours behind Auckland. Clocks go forward one hour between April and October.

TIPPING

Hotel and restaurant bills usually include tax and service in the form of a cover charge (called a couvert), but it is customary to round your bill up to the nearest 10kn and to leave an extra tip for exceptional service. Taxi drivers in the bigger cities sometimes round up the fare, so an additional tip is not always needed.

TOILETS

Toilets (*toalet* or WC) are usually marked *muški* for men and *ženski* for women.

TOURIST INFORMATION

The Croatia National Tourist Office (Hrvatska Turistička Zajednica) has offices in many countries. You can visit their website www. croatia.hr.
UK. 2 The Lanchesters, 162–164 Fulham Palace Road, London W6 9ER; tel: 020-8563 7979.

USA. Suite 4003, 350 Fifth Avenue, New York, NY 10118; tel: 212-279 8672.

There are local tourist offices throughout Croatia:

Baška: Kralja Zvonimir 114; tel: 051-856 817; www.tz-baska.hr.

Bol: Porat Bolskih Pomoraca bb; tel: 021-635 638; www.bol.hr.

Dubrovnik: Brsalje 5; tel: 020-321 011; www.tzdubrovnik.hr.

Grožnjan: Umberta Gorjana 3; tel: 052-776 131; www.tz-groznjan.hr.

Hvar: Trg Svetog Stjepana 16; tel: 021-741 059; www.tzhvar.hr.

Korčula Town: Obala Franje Tudjmana bb; tel: 020-715 701; www.visitkorcula.eu.

Krk Town: Vela Placa 1; tel: 051-221 414; www.tz-krk.hr.

Makarska: Obala kralja Tomislava 16; tel: 021-616 288; www.makarska-info.hr.

Mali Lošinj: Riva Lošinjskih Kapetana 29; tel: 051-231 884; www.tz-malilosinj.hr. **Motovun:** Trg Andrea Antico 1; tel: 052-681 726; www.istria-motovun.com.

Opatija: Vladimira Nazora 3; tel: 051-271 310; www.opatija-tourism.hr.

Osijek: Županijska 2; tel: 031-203 755; www.tzosijek.hr.

Poreč: Zagrebačka 9; tel: 052-451 293; www.to-porec.com.

Pula: Forum 3; tel: 052-219 197; www.pulainfo.hr.

Rab: Trg Municipium Arba 8; tel: 051-724 064; www.tzg-rab.hr.

Rijeka: Korzo 14; tel: 051-715 710; www.visitrijeka.hr.

Rovinj: Pina Budičina 12; tel: 052-811 566; www.tzgrovinj.hr.

Šibenik: Fausta Vrančića 18; tel: 022-212 075; www.sibenik-tourism.hr.

Split: Hrvatskog Narodnog Preporoda 7; tel: 021-348 600; www.visitsplit.com.

Trogir: Trg Ivana Pavla II 1; tel: 021-881 412; www.dalmacija.net/trogir.htm.

Varaždin: Ivana Padovca 3; tel: 042-210 987 www.tourism-varazdin.com.

Zadar: Svetog Leopolda Bogdana Mandića 1; tel: 023-315 316; www.zadar.hr.

Zagreb: Trg Bana Josip Jelačića 11; tel: 01-481 4051; www.zagreb-touristinfo.hr.

There are also tourist offices in many of Croatia's National Parks:

Brijuni: Brijunska 10, 52212 Fazana; tel: 052-525 888.

Kornati: Butina 2, 22243 Murter; tel: 022-435 740; www.kornati.hr.

Krka: Trg Ivana Pavla II 5, 22000 Šibenik; tel: 022-201 777; www.npkrka.hr.

Mljet: Pristanište 2, 20226 Govedari; tel: 020-744 041; www.np-mljet.hr.

Paklenica: Dr Franje Tuđmana 14a, 23244 Starigrad Paklenica; tel: 023-369 202; www.paklenica.hr.

Plitvice National Park: 53231 Plitvička Jezera; tel: 053-751 015; www.np-plitvicka-jezera.hr.

Risnjak: Bijela Voda 48, 51317 Crni Lug; tel: 051-836 133; www.risnjak.hr.

Sjeverni North Velebit: Obala Kralja Zvonimira 6, 53270 Senj; tel: 053-884 551; www.np-sjeverni-velebit.hr.

TRANSPORT

Buses. Croatia has an extensive local and national bus network. Tickets for local services should be bought from the driver or at a tobacco kiosk. Services generally operate daily 4am–11pm though in smaller towns and villages there may be no Sunday service.

Autotrans (tel: 051-660 300; www.autotrans.hr) is the main operator for long distance services. Tickets can be purchased from the local bus station or onboard. National bus services can be boarded at the bus stations or hailed at a designated stop. For information on long distance internal services, see www.akz.hr.

Taxis. Metered taxis can be found at ranks, hailed on the street or prebooked by telephone. A fixed-tariff list is displayed in many taxis, but it can be difficult to work out at what rate the meter is running so it is best to ask for an estimate of the fare in advance.

Trains. Rail travel is slow, with few direct connections between major towns and cities, and most Croatians do not travel by train. Tickets are cheap and can be purchased from railway stations or the onboard conductor. For train information, visit www.hznet.hr.

Trams. The cities of Zagreb and Osijek both have tram services that operate a similar timetable to the bus services. Tram tickets should be purchased from a tobacco kiosk and passengers have to validate tickets in the onboard machines.

By air. Regular domestic flights operated by Croatia Airlines connect Zagreb to Dubrovnik, Osijek, Pula, Rijeka, Split and Zadar.

By ferry. Jadrolinija (www.jadrolinija.hr) is the main car and passenger ferry operator in Croatia, with numerous routes along the Dalmatian coast and between the mainland and the islands.

Tickets must be purchased from the ticket office near the ferry dock prior to departure. In the summer months it is advisable to arrive in good time and buy vehicle tickets well in advance to minimise the risk of waiting in lengthy traffic queues to board a ferry. Foot passengers can usually purchase tickets just before their departure.

Where can I get a taxi? **Gdje ima taksija?**
What's the fare to…? **Koliko košta za…?**
When's the next bus to…? **Kada polazi slijedeći autobus za…?**
I want a ticket to… **Želim kartu za…**
single/return **u jednom smjeru/povratna**
Will you tell me when to get off? **Možete mi reći kad je moja stanica?**

VISAS AND ENTRY REQUIREMENTS

Any foreign national entering Croatia must possess a valid passport. For stays of less than 90 days, citizens of EU countries, the USA, Canada, Australia and New Zealand can enter Croatia without a visa. South Africans need a 90-day visa to visit Croatia.

Visitors to Croatia are required to register with the local police in each town or resort that they stay in, even if visiting friends or relatives. Hotels, campsites and travel agencies offering private accommodation automatically register guests. If you fail to register you may experience difficulties if you need to report anything to the police.

The **Consular Department of the Croatian Foreign Ministry** (tel: 01-456 9964, www.mvpei.hr) can provide further information, including a list of nationalities that require a visa to enter Croatia.

Currency restrictions. Foreign currency can be taken freely in and out of the country, but amounts over €10,000 must be declared. The import and export of *kuna* is restricted to 15,000kn.

Customs allowances. Visitors from other parts of the European Union have no limits on what they can import, as long as they can prove it is for personal use. Visitors from outside the EU can bring 2 litres of wine, 1 litre of spirits, 60 millilitres of perfume and 200 cigarettes without any duty being paid.

> I've nothing to declare **Nemam ništa za prijaviti**
> It's for my personal use **Ovo su moje stvari**

WEBSITES AND INTERNET ACCESS

Good websites for getting information before you go include the following:

www.croatia.hr The Croatian National Tourist Board provides lots of useful information, with details about accommodation, transport, national parks, current events, as well as an updated weather report.

www.vlada.hr The homepage of the Republic of Croatia contains general information about the country.

www.visit-croatia.co.uk Provides information about Croatia and its different regions. The site also has links to other useful websites and links to UK tour operators offering holidays in Croatia.

www.camping.hr The homepage of the Croatian Camping Union includes a useful contact number for prospective campers.

www.croatia-beaches.com A good site for finding the best beaches according to individual preferences.

www.croatiantimes.com English-language online newspaper covering general news as well as travel, business and sport.

Internet access. Most newer hotels, of three stars and above, now provide Wi-Fi for free, although a few insist on charging for it. Many cafés and restaurants offer free Wi-Fi, although in most cases you will need to ask for the code. The local tourist office will tell you where the nearest internet café is located.

YOUTH HOSTELS

Hostels affiliated to Hostelling International are normally prefixed YH and can be booked online at www.hfhs.hr. The guide price for a bed in a six-person dormitory is about 110kn; a single room is about 230kn.

Hostel Carpe Diem: Milana Šufflaya 3, Zagreb; tel: 01-468 0199; www.hostel.com.hr.

Hostel Jedro: Jadranska, Gradac; tel 021-697 240; www.hihostels.com.

Hostel Tufna: Franje Kuhača 10, Osijek; tel: 031-215 020 www.tufna.com.

YH Dubrovnik: Vinka Sagrestana 3; tel: 020-423 241; www.hfhs.hr.

YH Pula: Zaljev Valsaline 4; tel: 052-391 133; www.hihostels.com.

YH Rijeka: Šetalište XIII Divizije 23; tel: 051-406 420; www.hfhs.hr.

YH Zadar: Kneza Trpimira 76; tel: 023-331 145; www.hfhs.hr.

YH Zagreb: Petrinjska 77; tel: 01-484 1261; www.hfhs.hr.

Recommended Hotels

Until independence in 1991, large communist-era tourist resorts dominated Croatia's hotel scene. Since then, however, hotel facilities have been upgraded and there is a more diverse range of accommodation on offer, including boutique-style hotels, business-oriented accommodation and more welcoming family places to stay.

Most hotels levy a 30 percent surcharge for stays of less than 3 nights. Many hotels close between October and March, and high season rates generally apply in July and August. In the summer it's advisable to book your hotel in advance. Most hotels accept credit cards for making reservations, but travel agencies operating as booking agents for cheaper private accommodation will usually only take cash.

Most hotels advertise prices in euros, although they expect to be paid in kuna (at the time of writing, €1 = 7.65kn). These price guidelines are for a double room with bath in high season, including breakfast and tax:

$$$$	over 200 euros (1,530kn)
$$$	150–200 euros (1,147–1,530kn)
$$	100–150 euros (765–1,147kn)
$	under 100 euros (765kn)

CENTRAL AND EASTERN CROATIA

ZAGREB

Best Western Hotel Astoria $$$ *Petrinjska 71, 10000 Zagreb, tel: 01-480 8900, www.bestwestern.com.* Located between the railway station and the main square, this hotel reopened has a smart interior.

DoubleTree by Hilton $$$$ *Grada Vukovara 269a, 10000 Zagreb, tel: 01-600 1900, www.doubletree.com.* Near the Green Gold business district, this upmarket Hilton spin-off has spacious, elegant rooms and a well-equipped spa/gym area with indoor pool.

Dubrovnik $$$ *Gajeva 1, 10000 Zagreb, tel: 01-486 3555, www.hotel-dubrovnik.hr.* A stylish hotel in the heart of Zagreb with elegant guestrooms. Designer shops, trendy cafés and the city centre are just a few steps away.

Hotel Esplanade $$$$ *Mihanovićeva 1, 10000 Zagreb, tel: 01-456 6666, www.esplanade.hr.* One of Croatia's grandest hotels, the Esplanade used to be the rest stop for passengers on the *Orient Express*. It has a lovely Art Deco foyer, luxurious rooms, a health club and a casino.

Jägerhorn $$ *Ilica 14, 10000 Zagreb, tel: 01-483 3877, www.hotel-jagerhorn.hr.* Immensely charming hotel in an historic building near the main square, with romantic rooms surrounded by a pretty garden.

Palace Hotel $$$ *Trg Strossmayerov 10, 10000 Zagreb, tel: 01-489 9600, www.palace.hr.* The Palace was Zagreb's first hotel and it is noted for its fine Art-Deco facade. All rooms have a minibar, air-conditioning and satellite television.

OSIJEK

Hotel Osijek $$ *Šamačka 4, 31000 Osijek, tel: 031-230 333, www.hotelosijek.hr.* In a city with just a handful of tourist hotels, this high-rise hotel is still a good option. Well located on the banks of the Drava River, some of the rooms have great views. Facilities at the hotel include a gym, wellness centre and sauna.

Hotel Waldinger $$ *Županijska 8, 31000 Osijek, tel: 031-250 450, www.waldinger.hr.* Named after a local 19th century painter, this boutique hotel has three and four star options and a good wine cellar that offers tastings, as well as the perfect accompaniment to the excellent cuisine.

PLITVICE LAKES NATIONAL PARK

Hotel Jezero $$ *Plitvice Lakes National Park, 53231, tel: 053-751 400, www.np-plitvicka-jezera.hr.* It is well worth staying in the Plitvice Lakes National Park and this four-star hotel is as good a choice as any, despite the fact it's due for refurbishment. Facilities include a fitness centre and sauna. Book a room with a balcony overlooking the park.

MOTOVUN

Hotel Kaštel $$ *Trg Andrea Antico 7, 52424 Motovun, tel: 052-681 607*, www.hotel-kastel-motovun.hr. This former 18th-century palace, which also houses a spa, offers visitors a confortable place to stay. The rooms are done in a clean, contemporary style, many with extra beds and/or sofa beds. Many of the rooms have outstanding views of the countryside.

NOVIGRAD

Cittar Hotel $$ *Prolaz Venecija 1, 52466 Novigrad, tel: 052-757 737*, www.cittar.hr. Occupying a carefully refurbished building in the old town, close to the beach and the marina, this hotel has 14 rooms and a good restaurant.

POREČ

Grand Hotel Palazzo $$$$ *Obala Maršala Tita 24, 52440 Poreč, tel: 052-858 500*, www.hotel-palazzo.hr. This 70-room four-star hotel has a commanding position by the water on the main seaside promenade. A spa, pool restaurant and marina are all nearby.

Hotel Poreč $$ *Rade Končara 1, 52440 Poreč, tel: 052-451 811*, www.hotelporec.com. Located in front of the bus station, this hotel offers reasonably priced, comfortable rooms as well as good sports facilities including tennis, golf, diving and water-skiing.

Valamar Diamant Hotel $$$ *Brulo bb, 52440 Poreč, tel: 052-408 800*, www.valamar.com/diamant-hotel-porec. Lying a 20-minute walk east of the old town and with good views overlooking the sea, this large, modern hotel has excellent facilities, including indoor and outdoor pools, tennis courts and a luxurious health and beauty centre.

PULA

Hotel Scaletta $$ *Flavijevska 26, 52100 Pula, tel: 052-541 025,* www.hotel-scaletta.com. Close to the Roman amphitheatre, this small family-run hotel has 12 cheerfully decorated rooms and a highly regarded restaurant.

Valsabbion $$$ *Pješčana Uvala IX/26, 52100 Pula, tel: 052-218 033,* www.valsabbion.hr. This ultra-fashionable hotel, located on Pula's marina, has modern, tasteful rooms with air-conditioning and a minibar. The hotel also has a small pool.

ROVINJ

Hotel Adriatic $$$ *Obala Pino Budicin bb, 52210 Rovinj, tel: 052-815 088,* www.maistra.hr. Occupying an old townhouse on the central square in Rovinj, Adriatic has 27 well-furnished rooms, with air-conditioning, minibar, satellite television and gorgeous sea views.

Hotel Lone $$$$ *Luje Adamovića, 52210 Rovinj, tel: 052-800 250,* www.lonehotel.com. This sleek, five-star member of the Design Hotels group sits in the lush greenery of the Zlatni Rt forest park. Its spacious, modern rooms have views of the park and the large indoor pool and spa complex.

KVARNER GULF

OPATIJA

Milenij $$$$ *Maršala Tita 109, 51410 Opatija, tel: 051-202 000,* www.milenijhotel.hr. Opatija's premier hotel has a prime position on the Lungomare, with luxurious rooms, a heated outdoor pool and a bustling seafront café.

Hotel Mozart $$$ *Maršala Tita 138, 51410 Opatija, tel: 051-718 260,* www.hotel-mozart.hr. This small and elegant hotel, built in the late 19th century, has just 27 guest rooms and three suites. All of the rooms are light and airy, with modern bathrooms. Superior and deluxe rooms have balconies.

PAKLENICA NATIONAL PARK

Hotel Vicko $$ *Joze Dokoze 20, 23244 Starigrad Paklenica, tel: 023-369 304*, www.hotel-vicko.hr. The Vicko is an agreeable family-run hotel with a wide range of facilities, including a highly regarded restaurant. Some of the hotel rooms have sea views. Its sister hotel, Villa Vicko, is only a few metres away, with sea-facing rooms.

RIJEKA

Hotel Continental $ *Šetalište Andrije Kačića-Miošića 1, 51000 Rijeka, tel: 051-372 008*, www.jadran-hoteli.hr. This pleasant two-star hotel is beside the city's canal, a 15-minute walk from town. En-suite rooms are clean and functional. The hotel's café also sells delicious ice cream.

Grand Hotel Bonavia $$$ *Dolac 4, 51000 Rijeka, tel: 051-357 100*, www.bonavia.hr. This four-star business hotel has spacious, comfortable and classically styled rooms and a spa and gym. It enjoys a prime location in the heart of the shopping and financial district.

THE ISLANDS

Hotel Apoksiomen $$ *Riva Lošinjskih kapetana 1, 51550 Mali Lošinj, tel: 051-520 820*, www.apoksiomen.com. Located in a refurbished building in the old town, overlooking the seafront promenade, this reasonable four-star hotel has 25 rooms, some with balconies.

Hotel Corinthia-Baš**ka $$** *Emila Geistlicha 38, 51523 Baška, Krk, tel: 051-656 111*, www.hotelibaska.hr. There are in fact five Baska hotels and villa units, all located just metres from one of Croatia's best beaches. The Corinthia has the best choice of rooms and arguably provides best value for money. A wellness centre and pool complex are amongst the extensive choice of facilities on offer.

Grand Hotel Imperial $$ *M de Dominsia 9, 51280 Rab, tel: 051-724 522*, www.imperial.hr. Located in Rab Town's leafy park, the Imperial has light, spacious and well-furnished rooms with views over the sea or the park. Three tennis courts and a mini-golf course.

DALMATIA

DUBROVNIK

Bellevue $$$$ *Pera Čingrije 7, 20000 Dubrovnik, tel: 020-330 000*, www.hotel-bellevue.hr. This five-star luxury boutique hotel is set in a spectacular cliff-top location with fine views over the bay.

Excelsior Hotel $$$$ *Frana Supila 12, 20000 Dubrovnik, tel: 020-353 353*, www.hotel-excelsior.hr. This venerable five-star hotel has a superb position, just a 10-minute walk from Dubrovnik's old town. The rooms provide dramatic views.

Hotel Lapad $$$$ *Lapadska Obala 37, 20000 Dubrovnik, tel: 020-455 555*, www.hotel-lapad.hr. Overlooking Gruž harbour, 3km from the old town, this elegant hotel has 193 rooms and outdoor pool. A taxi boat takes guests to nearby beaches.

Pucić Palace $$$$ *Od Puča 1, 20000 Dubrovnik, tel: 020-326 222*, www.thepucicpalace.com. One of only a handful of hotels within Dubrovnik's old town, with 19 deluxe rooms, large bathrooms and lots of attention to detail.

MAKARSKA

Biokovo $$ *Kralja Tomislava bb, 21300 Makarska, tel: 021-615 244*, www.hotelbiokovo.hr. The Biokovo has a prime location on Makarska's seafront promenade, with comfortable rooms. Try to book a room with a sea view.

Hotel Makarska $$$ *Potok 17, 21300 Makarska, tel: 021-616 360*, www.makarska-hotel.com. More like a *pension* than a hotel, with some very small rooms, the Makarska doesn't offer great value for money. Parking and good views over the Biokovo Mountains are its more redeeming features.

MALI STON

Vila Koruna $ *Pelješki put 1, 20234 Mali Ston, tel: 020-754 999,* www.vila-koruna.hr. This restaurant-with-rooms provides basic but comfortable accommodation. The highlight of this peaceful location is the exquisite seafood for which Mali Ston is renowned.

ŠIBENIK

Hotel Jadran $ *Obala Tuđmana 52, 22000 Šibenik, tel: 022-242 000,* www.rivijera.hr. The 57 rooms in this purpose-built hotel are surprisingly still the only hotel option in town. Its prime seafront location goes a little way to compensate for its ugly façade and average rooms.

Solaris Beach Resort $$$ *Hoteli Solaris 86, 22000 Šibenik, tel: 022-361 001,* www.solaris.hr. This large holiday resort, located 6km (4 miles) out of town, offers five hotels (Hotel Ivan is the best), apartments, a campsite and its own marina. Its attractive setting, enormous wellness centre and large number of indoor and outdoor pools compensate for the impersonal feel of the resort. There is a regular shuttle service to the town centre.

SPLIT

Le Méridien Grand Hotel Lav $$$ *Grljevaćka 2A, Podstrana, 21000 Split, tel: 021-500 500,* www.lemeridien.com. Though 9km (6 miles) outside Split, you can arrive there by water-taxi from the airport. It was the first and is still the best of Split's crop of luxury hotels. The Diocletian spa, infinity pool, casino, marina and sunken champagne bar are just a few of the facilities to be enjoyed.

Hotel Slavija $$$ *Buvinina 2, 21000 Split, tel: 021-323 840,* www. hotelslavija.com. This hotel has an unbeatable location at the heart of the historic Diocletian's Palace. The hotel has 24 rooms, many with small balconies. However, a stay here is not for everyone, as the music from the surrounding bars plays loudly during the summer months.

Hotel Vestibul Palace $$$$ *Iza Vestibula 4, 21000 Split, tel: 021-329 329*, www.vestibulpalace.com. This chic boutique hotel has just seven rooms in an old stone house near the vestibule of Diocletian's Palace. Polished wood, glass and natural light blend with Roman stone walls to create an intriguing mix of ancient and modern. Additional facilities are limited by the size of the building.

OMIŠ

Villa Dvor $$ *Mosorska 13, Omiš, tel: 021-863 444*, www.hotel-villa dvor.hr. A lift takes guests from the car park to the top of the hill where this boutique hotel perches. Four of the 23 comfortable rooms have a loggia from which you can take in glorious views of the sea.

THE ISLANDS

Hotel Kaštil $$ *Frane Radiča 1, 21420 Bol, Brač, tel: 021-635 995*, www.kastil.hr. Overlooking the harbour, this old stone building has 32 rooms with minimalist style furnishing, plus two lively restaurants and a cocktail bar.

Lešić-Dimitri Palace $$$$ *Don Pavle Pože 1-6 20260 Korčula, tel: 020-715 560*, www.lesic-dimitri.com. This elegant – and very expensive – five-star has bags of charm and atmosphere as it is housed in an 18th-century bishop's palace and five medieval cottages.

Martinis Marchi $$$$ *Maslinica, 21430 Šolta, tel: 021-572 768*, www.martinis-marchi.com. The German owners have transformed the interior of this 18th century Baroque castle. The largest of the six sumptuous suites stretches upwards over the five floors of the tower, and all surround the courtyard, the centrepiece of which is a heated outdoor pool.

Hotel Podstine $$$$ *Put Podstina 11, 21450 Hvar, tel: 021-740 400,* www.podstine.com. This hotel has a peaceful seafront location just 15 minutes' walk from Hvar Town. It has comfortable rooms, most with a good view and balcony. The hotel also has a private beach, arboretum and restaurant.

Hotel San Giorgio $$$ *Petra Hektorovića 2, 21480 Vis, tel: 021-711 362,* www.hotelsangiorgiovis.com. This friendly hotel combines comfortable, contemporary rooms with an excellent restaurant and on-site winery. You can even stay at the hotel's private lighthouse, which is a short boat ride away. All rooms require a minimum week's stay.

TROGIR

Hotel Concordia $$$ *Bana Berislavića 22, 21220 Trogir, tel: 021-885 400,* www.concordia-hotel.htnet.hr. The rooms are simply furnished in this otherwise attractive 300-year-old family-run hotel right on the promenade at Trogir. The waterside café is an extra pleasure.

Hotel Palace $$$ *Put Gradine, 21220 Trogir, tel: 021-685 555,* www. hotel-palace.net. Purpose built and a 10-minute walk from the centre of town, the Palace offers modern and comfortable rooms with balconies, some with a sea view. Easy parking makes a welcome change from the fight for spaces in Trogir old town in high summer.

ZADAR

Art Hotel Kalelarga $$$ *Majke Margarite 3, 23000 Zadar, tel: 023-233 000,* www.arthotel-kalelarga.com. The only other high-quality (and slightly cheaper) accommodation in the heart of the old town is this elegant boutique hotel with exposed stone walls. It does seem to have every shade of beige imaginable, but the result is soothing.

Hotel Bastion $$$$ *Bedemi Zadarska pobuna 13, 23000 Zadar, tel: 023-494 950,* www.hotel-bastion.hr. Plenty of thought has been given to this four-star hotel's interior design around the old stone walls of the historic bastion. It also has very good spa facilities and an atmospheric terrace restaurant.

INDEX

Accommodation 112
Airports 113

Baška 57
Bicycle Hire 114
Biograd 64
Biševo 80
Borik 64
Brač 76
    Bol 76
    Hermitage Blaca 77
    Žlatni Rat 76
Brela 70
Brijuni Islands 49
Budgeting for Your Trip
    114
Buzet 51

Camping 115
Car Hire 115
Cavtat 76
Climate 116
Cres Town 58
Crime and Safety 116
Cultural Performances 94

Đakovo 39
Dalmatia 59
Diving 83
Driving 117
Drvenik 70
Dubrovnik 70
    cathedral 75
    Dubrovnik Festival
        76
    Great Fountain of
        Onofrio 73
    Luža Square 73
    medieval walls 73
    Orlando's Column 74
    Pile Gate 73
    Ploče Gate 73
    Rector's Palace 75
    Small Fountain of
        Onofrio 73
    Sponza Palace 73
    St Blaise church 74
    Stradun 73
    War Photo Limited 75

Elaphite Islands 81
Electricity 118
Embassies and Consulates
    119
Emergencies 119
Etnoland 63

Football 85

Gay and Lesbian
    Travellers 119
Grožnjan 51
Guides and Tours 120

Health and Medical
    Care 121
Holidays 126
Homeland War Museum
    76
Hum 52
Hvar 77
    Hvar Town 77

Istria 41

Kaštela 69
Kopački rit Nature
    Park 39
Korčula 80
    Korčula Town 80
    Marco Polo House 80
    St Mark's Cathedral
        80
Kornati Islands National
    Park 65
Krapanj 66
Krapinske Toplice 37
Krk 56
Krka National Park 64
Kvarner Gulf 52

Labin 48
Lake Jarun 35
Language 121
Limski Zaljev 49
loggia 64
Lokrum 76
Lošinj 59
Lovran 55

Makarska 70
Makarska Riviera 69
Mali Lošinj 59
Mljet 80
    Mljet National
        Park 80
    St Mary's Island 81
Money 123
Motovun 50

Novalja 58
Novigrad 48

Omiš 69
Opatija 54
Opatija Riviera 54
Opening Hours 124
Osijek 39, 40

Pag 58
Pag Town 58
Paklenica National
    Park 56
Pazin 50
Pelješac Peninsula 70
Plitvice Lakes National
    Park 37
Podgora 70
Police 125
Poreč 46
    Basilica of Euphrasius
        47
    Romanesque House 47
Postal Services 125
Prvič 66
Public Transport 129
Pula 42
    Cathedral of St
        Mary 43
    Roman Amphitheatre
        42
    Roman Forum 43
    Temple of Augustus 43
    Triumphal Arch of
        Sergius 43

Rab 57
Rabac 48
Rijeka 53
    Our Lady of Trsat
        church 54
    Stari Grad 54

St Vitus 54
    Trsat castle 54
Roški Slap 65
Rovinj 44
    Grisia 46
    Heritage Museum 45
    Rovinj Aquarium 45
    St Euphemia 44

Sailing 84
Salona 68
Senj 56
Shopping 87
Šibenik 62
    Bunari – Secrets of
        Šibenik 63
    Falconry Centre 63
    garden of St
        Lawrence's
        Monastery 63
    Šibenik Cathedral 62
Skradin 65
Skradinski Buk 65
Slavonia 38, 39
Solaris 64
Šolta 78
Split 66
    Bačvice 68
    Cathedral of St
        Domnius 67
    Diocletian's Palace 66
    Golden Gate 67
    Marmontova 68
    Meštrović Gallery 68
    Peristyle 67
    Split Gallery of
        Modern Art 68
    Zenta 68
Ston 70

Telephones 126
Tennis 86
Time Zones 127
Tipping 127
Tourist Information 127
Trakošćan Castle 36
Trogir 64
    cathedral 64
    Čipiko Palace 64
    Kamerlengo Castle 64
Tučepi 70
Tvrđa 40

Učka Mountains 55
Umag 48

Varaždin 35
Veliki Tabor 37
Veli Lošinj 59
Vis 78
    Komiža 79
    Maritime Museum
        80
    Vis Town 78
Visas and Entry
    Requirements 130
Visovac 65
Vodice 64
Vodnjan 44
Voloska 55
Vrsar 48
Vukovar 41

Walking, Hiking and
    Climbing 86
Watersports 84
Websites and Internet
    Cafes 131
Where to Shop 90

Youth Hostels 132

Zadar 60
   Archaeological
      Museum 61
   Narodni Trg 61
   Široka Ulica 60
   St Donat's Church 61
   St Simeon church 61
   Town Loggia 61
   Zadar Cathedral 62
   Zadar Museum of
      Antique Glass 62
Zagorje 35
Zagreb 27

Art Pavilion 28
Botanical Gardens 34
Dolac Market 31
Lisinski Concert
   Hall 34
Lotrščak Tower 31
Maksimir Park 34
Meštrović Atelier 33
Mimara 29
Museum Of Arts and
   Crafts 28
Museum of Broken
   Relationships 32
Museum of Contem-
   porary Art 34

National Library 34
statue of King
   Tomislav 28
St Mark's Church 33
Strossmayer Gallery 28
Strossmayer Parade 32
Tkalčićeva 33
Trg Bana Josip Jelačića
   30
Zagreb Cathedral 30
Zagreb City Museum
   33
Zagreb Zoo 35
Zaostrog 70
Zlarin 66

Berlitz® pocket guide

Croatia

Fourth Edition 2014

Written by Robin McKelvie
Updated by Mary Novakovich
Edited by Catherine Dreghorn
Picture Editor: Tom Smyth
Art Editor: Shahid Mahmood
Series Editor: Tom Stainer
Production: Tynan Dean and Rebeka Davies

Photography credits: AKG 19, 20; Alamy 82, 101; Bigstock 3TC, 12, 26, 34, 49, 55; Corrie Wingate/Apa Publications 2TL, 2/3M, 4ML, 7MC, 11, 31, 32, 38/39, 48, 50, 51, 52, 69, 81, 89, 90, 99, 102; Dominic Burdon/APA Publications 2TC, 2/3T, 2/3M, 4TL, 4/5M, 4/5T, 5TC, 6ML, 6ML, 7MC, 7TC, 8, 29, 30, 33, 36, 37, 41, 44, 45, 50, 46, 58, 60, 63, 65, 66, 67, 70, 71, 72, 77, 78/79, 85, 87, 91; Dreamstime 14, 24, 42; Getty 22, 93; Gregory Wrona/Apa Publications 1, 2MC, 2ML, 2/3M 5MC, 6TL, 97; iStockphoto 4ML, 4MR, 16, 53, 56; Jo Mercer/ Apa Publications 74, 94; Mark Read/Apa Publications 16, 17
Cover picture: Corrie Wingate/Apa Publications

Every effort has been made to provide accurate information in this publication, but changes are inevitable. The publisher cannot be responsible for any resulting loss, inconvenience or injury.

Contact us

At Berlitz we strive to keep our guides as accurate and up to date as possible, but if you find anything that has changed, or if you have any suggestions on ways to improve this guide, then we would be delighted to hear from you.

Berlitz Publishing, PO Box 7910,
London SE1 1WE, England.
email: berlitz@apaguide.co.uk
www.insightguides.com/berlitz